D1289023

From MOTHER *With* LOVE

A treasury of recipes for cooking and living

Rebecca Stewart Wight and Selma Wight Beard

PEACHTREE PUBLISHERS, LTD.

Published by
PEACHTREE PUBLISHERS, LTD.
494 Armour Circle, N.E.
Atlanta, Georgia 30324

Copyright © 1984 Selma Wight Beard

Design by Cynthia Davis

Cover photo by Terri Teague

All rights reserved. No part of this book may be reproduced in any form
or by any means without the prior written permission of the Publisher,
excepting brief quotes used in connection with reviews, written specifically
for inclusion in a magazine or newspaper.

Manufactured in the United States of America

First printing

Library of Congress Catalog Number 84-60924

ISBN: 0-931948-64-9

To Selma and Bobby, who brought
this out of the attic.

FOREWORD

Unique expressions of love are truly timeless. And perhaps none is so treasured or so universally understood as that of a mother for her child. This book is a record of one such mother's gentle wisdom and zest for life and the special vehicle through which she passes on her talent for happiness to a child who is far away from home. These letters contain not only the ingredients for good eating, but also some rare ingredients for good living. I hope that they may prove useful and enjoyable to others, as well.

Rebecca Stewart was born in Marietta, Georgia, in 1894. She grew up in Athens where her father was a professor at the University of Georgia. After undergraduate and post-graduate work in domestic science, she taught home economics for three years at the University of Georgia. In 1914, Rebecca Stewart became Mrs. Ward Wight and the couple settled in Atlanta where they raised five children.

I am one of those children, and I am the befuddled would-be cook to whom these letters are mercifully addressed. In 1941, I married a dashing young Marine aviator and was abruptly transported away from my family and my mother's legendary cooking into the exciting and yet often lonely and disconcerting life of a World War II bride.

Suddenly I found myself all alone in the role of "chief cook and bottle washer" with only limited cooking experience and in great need of guidance. My subsequent desperate search through various cookbooks only left my head spinning. It was then that I dispatched a sad little SOS home, and it was Mother who came most competently to my rescue.

The following text is based on the crash course in cooking — and in living — with which my mother provided me during 1942 and 1943. My husband says he never ate as good again as he did that first year we were married! Mother's cooking was special because it maintained the elements of basic Southern dishes while combining and complementing them in ways that were always original and delicious.

My mother passed away in 1977, but a part of her lives on in the many gifts of love which she shared with her children. This cookbook is one such gift, and the sentiments expressed within it surely are not so different from those which passed between many mothers and daughters during those years. I hope that as other daughters of that time read these pages, memories of similar advice and assistance received from their own mothers will seem more vivid. (Perhaps someone may even bring out their own special "Mother's Recipe" for dinner tonight.) My experiences were similar to those of thousands of the young war brides, and these letters and others like them lovingly attempted to smooth the rough road we travelled.

Selma Wight Beard
September, 1984

From Mother With Love

Atlanta, Georgia
June 13, 1942

Selma darling:

When your little blue missive came this morning, I was not sure whether to laugh or cry over the account of your pitiful, heart-breaking struggle to keep house and cook for Dick. I feel certainly to blame and am humbled with shame that I should have let my child go forth into the world to do a job she was not equipped to do.

Of course I understand why you found the cookbook confusing — cookbooks are built upon the principle that the user understands the rudiments of cookery — and while I did think you knew enough to start, from watching Bella and me, I realize now that we just took too much for granted. Cooking has definitely become a scientific art.

Bella and I had a good laugh over the way you described our cooking — "A dash of everything in the kitchen and out comes a heavenly dessert!" Obviously, you didn't understand the finer points if that is the way it seemed to you. But how could I teach you when you led such a hectic life? All through high school you were constantly on the move — at home only long enough to change clothes and sleep. Then you were off to college with only a few gay weekends at home, followed by debut and marriage. And there were so many things to learn — music, art, swimming, horseback, dancing, etc., besides an education. I guess I'm not too much to blame, but I shall make up for my negligence by giving you a "Mail Order Course" beginning *now*. File these letters and someday you'll have quite a collection.

Daddy and I were thrilled that Dick was able to find such a lovely apartment, so nicely furnished, and we are shipping some of your wedding gifts so you can really feel at home. Miami is such a lovely place to live and a perfect place to learn to cook

because of the great varieties of available foods.

It is also a place where entertaining is almost a requisite, and I know that Dick will want to bring his buddies from Opalocka home for dinner many evenings. So be ready for him, darling. A man takes great pride in the fact that his wife can "toss up" a swell meal on short notice (and justly, because so few can) and likes nothing better than to show off before his friends. It's grand, too, provided you can measure up to his expectations, because if you can get the crowd to come to your house, you've learned one of the greatest secrets of a happy marriage.

First things first. See that you have these few pieces of **KITCHEN EQUIPMENT**. With these you can make any recipe I send you. Since Dick will probably be moved every few months, you should probably buy your utensils at the dime store so that you may abandon the less important ones if you have to move in a hurry. The simpler you keep your kitchen, the better. Too many implements are so much "impedimenta."

Set of measuring spoons
Wire whisk
Spatula
Sharp butcher knife
Paring knife
Long-handled spoon
Long-handled fork
Measuring cups (2)
Apple corer
Potato ball spoon
Tea Strainer
Colander
Large strainer
8-inch tin pan with 2-inch sides
Muffin tins
Covered skillet

Small skillet for eggs
Double boiler
Sauce pans (3 sizes)
Large covered boiler
Biscuit pan
Pie pan
Casserole (pyrex)
2 molds (1 quart, 1 pint)
Custard cups or ramekins
3 mixing bowls
Grater
Coffee pot
Tea pot

I know exactly how your dressing table looks — great jars of fragrant cold creams, powders in all shades, toilet waters, lipsticks, rouges, nail enamels — all the necessary ingredients for a well-groomed appearance, all of which I approve without reservation. But I ask you, what price a lovely wife who serves unpalatable meals?

What I am driving at is simply this: You think nothing of paying three dollars for a lipstick, but you are going to faint when you see this next list of **ACCESSORIES TO GOOD COOKING**, which I insist that you buy and replace when they give out. It is only by having these essentials on hand that you can possibly make delectable dishes. Unless you are willing to skimp somewhere else in order to buy these things, you'd better just give Dick ham and eggs every night! So get them and let's start cooking.

I realize that war restrictions will limit this list from time to time, but be not discouraged. Let ingenuity and common sense guide your selections and who knows what new and tempting dishes you may create.

Chili powder   Horseradish
Curry powder   Vinegar
Bay leaves   Cooking oil

Flour	Pepper sauce
Meal	Garlic
Sugar	Lemons
Coffee	Capers
Tea	Catsup
Rice	Olives
Grits	Chili sauce
Canned milk	Mayonnaise
Almond extract	Raisins
Vanilla extract	Nuts
Lemon extract	Cocoa
Crème de cacao	Unsweetened
Cooking wine	chocolate
Rum	Cornstarch
Pepper	Gelatin
Salt	Vegetable coloring
Mustard	B.V. extract
Cinnamon	Toothpicks
Paprika	

You say you can't even scramble an egg! Mama says that when she married she couldn't even boil water, so I guess each generation is improving at that.

The strange fact is that it is more difficult to scramble eggs nicely than it is to make a Baked Alaska. I wouldn't be surprised if there weren't more improperly scrambled eggs served in America than any other dish. So master the art at once, even if you waste a whole dozen eggs in the process. And experiment during the day so the failures can be dumped in the garbage. That sounds extravagant, but just at this point I have more respect for Dick's stomach than for his purse. Remember Seneca said, "If you're surprised at the number of our maladies, count our cooks." One other thing — only the best eggs are worth buying. In some countries the older the eggs, the better, but we're not living in those benighted places.

For perfect **SCRAMBLED EGGS** for 2, put 1 Tbl.

Scrambled Eggs

1 Tbl. cooking oil	2 Tbl. water
3 (or 4) eggs	salt

cooking oil in your little aluminum skillet and place over slow heat. Break 3 (or 4) eggs in a bowl and add 2 Tbl. water. With a fork, beat eggs until well-mixed but not foamy. By now, your skillet is hot. Pour the eggs in, and as they begin to curl around the edges, take a spoon and slowly turn those edges in on the uncooked part. Repeat this as each new edge cooks, until finally all will be folded and they'll be as light as a summer cloud. Do not salt until cooked. Salt changes both color and texture.

If you want to cook proper **FRIED EGGS** (sunny-side-up), try this method. Place a small amount of bacon drippings, oil, or butter in the frying pan. When hot, but not yet sizzling, break eggs into pan, being careful not to break yolks. Add 1 Tbl. of water and cover tightly. In a jiffy, your eggs are perfect.

To vary your breakfasts, give him **FRENCH TOAST** and bacon. Melt a small amount of butter in skillet. Beat an egg with a dash of milk and salt. Dip your slices of bread in this mixture and brown. He'll love it! One egg should make 4 slices of toast.

For **CINNAMON TOAST**, toast one side of bread in oven and remove. Spread untoasted side with melted butter, honey or sugar, and cinnamon. Return to oven and toast.

To make your **DADDY'S FAVORITE TOAST**, toast buttered bread on both sides. Place thick slices of tomato on each piece of toast. Cover generously with American or cheddar cheese and return to oven until cheese is melted. Serve with crisp bacon or sausage.

For goodness sake, don't give Dick the same breakfast every morning. Get up in time to have a gay breakfast, one that will start life off with the good old "wim and wigor" he will need to fly Uncle Sam's planes all day!

Use bright linens, colorful china, and perky, saucy-looking centerpieces. Don't look in books for cute arrangements — look in your own brain and in the great outdoors.

Fried Eggs

| bacon drippings, | 2 eggs |
| oil, or butter | 1 Tbl. water |

French Toast

butter	dash of salt
1 egg	4 slices of bread
dash of milk	

Cinnamon Toast

| 2 slices of bread | honey (or sugar) |
| melted butter | cinnamon |

Daddy's Favorite Toast

2 slices of bread,	American or
buttered	cheddar cheese
tomato slices	slices

I always felt that the aromas of breakfast cooking were a wonderful accompaniment to a man's morning ablutions and dressing. A husband who has been drinking in the fragrance of bacon broiling or ham frying, or the spicy odor of cinnamon toast mingled with the aroma of hot coffee, could never come to the breakfast table in any mood other than that of peace with the world and a zest for living.

Be sure to serve fruits (whether juices or stewed, fresh or canned, melons or grapes) and then a cereal (either prepared or cooked). Add to this an egg, and crisp bacon, sausage, or ham, with toast or hot cakes, and you have a hearty beakfast fit for a king.

Vary eggs and toast with cheese, chipped beef, or tomatoes, or even add leftover rice to your scrambled eggs. Most men like mullet roe or salt mackerel for breakfast as well.

Perfect **FRYING** requires instant high heat — an even spread of heat under the skillet. The trick in frying is to seal the surface of the food immediately with hot fat, so that in further cooking, only the heat and not the fat will penetrate. Frying has come into disrepute because too often temperatures are not right. If fat is too hot, it breaks down into harmful compounds; if not hot enough, it soaks into the food rendering it less digestible. With care, however, you may serve digestible as well as delicious fried foods. The following recipes are excellent for breakfast or for lunch.

For **HASH BROWNS,** put a small amount of bacon drippings in a skillet. When hot, add 2 cups finely-chopped, boiled potatoes, salt, and pepper. When browned on the bottom, turn and brown other side. Turn into a platter and serve at once.

To prepare **FRENCH FRIES,** peel potatoes, slice in small strips, and soak in cold, salted water. Drain, dry, and fry in deep cooking oil hot enough to brown a 1-inch cube of bread in 20 seconds. When brown, drain on paper and salt to taste.

For **FISH CAKES,** mix 1½ cups cooked fish with 1½

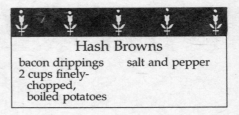

Hash Browns

bacon drippings	salt and pepper
2 cups finely-chopped, boiled potatoes	

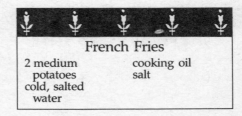

French Fries

2 medium potatoes	cooking oil
cold, salted water	salt

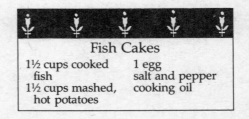

Fish Cakes

1½ cups cooked fish	1 egg
1½ cups mashed, hot potatoes	salt and pepper
	cooking oil

cups hot mashed potatoes. Beat 1 egg slightly and add to this. Add salt and pepper. Shape into cakes. Fry in hot cooking oil until brown. Serves 2 generously.

Bacon and Sausage are simple as can be. Arrange strips of **BACON** on racks in broiler, place under flame, and broil until crisp. Remove and drain. For small breakfast links, broil **SAUSAGE** in same way, but if larger links, cook in covered frying pan over medium heat with 1 Tbl. water added, until browned and well done.

For **BAKING POWDER BISCUITS,** first preheat oven to 450°. Then sift together 2 cups flour, 2 tsp. baking powder, and 1 tsp. salt. Cut in 4 Tbl. shortening and 1 cup sweet milk. Knead slightly, roll, cut out with biscuit cutter, and prick with fork. Bake 12 to 15 minutes. Start on lower rack and move to top rack to brown. Makes two dozen biscuits.

For **POPOVERS,** preheat oven to 475°. Next, beat 2 eggs until light, and add ¼ tsp. salt, 1 cup flour, 1 Tbl. melted butter or oil, and 1 cup milk (a little at a time). Beat until smooth, making a very thin batter. Grease popover pans and fill each cup ½ full or less. Place in center of oven. Cook 15 minutes, then reduce heat to 350° and continue baking 15 or 20 minutes, until dry and crisp. Do not open oven for first 10 minutes, so they will pop well. Makes 8 to 12 popovers.

Preheat oven to 450° for **TWIN MOUNTAIN MUFFINS.** Then cream 1 cup butter. Add ¼ cup sugar, and 1 slightly beaten egg. Sift 2 cups flour with 4 tsp. baking powder and a dash of salt. Alternate flour mixture with ¼ cup milk, adding to butter-sugar mixture until all is used. Bake in buttered muffin tins for 20 minutes. Makes 12 muffins.

For **COCOA,** scald ½ cup milk in double boiler. Mix ½ Tbl. sugar with ½ Tbl. cocoa. Stir ½ cup boiling water into the cocoa mixture slowly and boil 1 or 2 minutes. Pour into scalding milk and beat with rotary beater. This makes 1 cup. Increase proportions according to number of people you wish to serve.

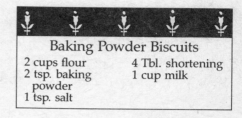

Baking Powder Biscuits

2 cups flour	4 Tbl. shortening
2 tsp. baking powder	1 cup milk
1 tsp. salt	

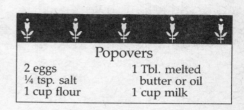

Popovers

2 eggs	1 Tbl. melted butter or oil
¼ tsp. salt	
1 cup flour	1 cup milk

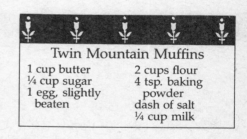

Twin Mountain Muffins

1 cup butter	2 cups flour
¼ cup sugar	4 tsp. baking powder
1 egg, slightly beaten	dash of salt
	¼ cup milk

Cocoa

½ cup milk	½ cup boiling water
½ Tbl. sugar	
½ Tbl. cocoa	

For **COFFEE,** use 1 rounded Tbl. coffee to 1 cup water per person. Add an extra spoon for the pot if you have plenty of coffee. For percolator, use medium grind, for drip pot and vacuum coffeemaker, use pulverized coffee. Measure coffee and water carefully, don't overperk. Try not to reheat, as it's better when fresh.

For **FLUFFY OMELETTE,** separate 4 eggs, and beat yolks until thick and lemon-colored. Add salt and pepper and 4 Tbl. hot water, milk, or cream. (Water makes it more tender.) Beat whites until stiff. Cut and fold into yolk mixture. Melt butter or bacon drippings in heavy omelette or frying pan. Turn mixture into pan and cook over medium heat until well puffed and evenly browned on bottom. Omelette should cook until firm to the touch. It may be cooked the last few minutes in a medium oven to brown top. Fold and serve at once. Serves 2. If desired this may be served with Spanish Sauce (see pg. 29-30), or with mushrooms, chicken hash (see pg. 9), seafoods, etc.

Perhaps this is as good a time as any to tell you about the advantages of leftovers. You can save yourself hours of time in both shopping and preparing food if you will buy more meat than you need for one meal. It takes just as long to buy and cook a 2 lb. roast or a tiny chicken as it does to cook a 6 lb. roast or a 6 lb. hen. The smaller ones are gone at one meal, while the larger may be stored in the ice box and used a hundred delicious ways.

This same principle holds true with many different foods. Make enough white sauce for several times, enough salad dressing for a week, enough waffle batter for a week. Always cook a little extra rice and save a piece of pie crust or biscuit dough. The recipes for these will have to come in another letter but I do want you to learn to be happy over some leftovers in your ice box, because these cut

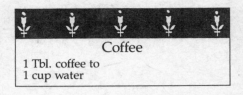

Coffee

1 Tbl. coffee to
1 cup water

Fluffy Omelette

4 eggs
salt and pepper

4 Tbl. hot water,
milk, or cream
butter or bacon
drippings

down your working hours and pot washing, and leave many more hours for sunshine and fun.

Back to the leftover meats: Chop up about ½ cup and add to your eggs for an omelette. Or, to create a super **HASH,** add a diced potato and a slice of onion to some stock, and drop in a little of the chopped meat. Cook about 10 minutes and you have a savory hash to serve with grits or on toast or waffles. (Thicken if needed, with 1 Tbl. flour mixed in a little water.) This dish has come into disrepute because it has been so mistreated and such awful concoctions have been passed off as hash, but real hash is as fine a dish as any man could want.

I remember my father told me that he never had a breakfast at the Governor's Mansion when Terrell [Governor Joseph Meriwether Terrel (1902-1907)] was the chief executive that turkey hash and waffles were not served.

So try to manage hash as often as you can. Keep a jar of B.V. extract on hand and add a teaspoon to your hash for extra flavor if your stock is low.

MEAT BISCUITS, one of our favorite breakfasts, is made from leftovers. Toast leftover biscuits, butter, and arrange on a platter. Pile chopped, leftover meat (chicken, roast, or chipped beef) on the biscuit, top with grated cheese, and run under broiler until cheese is melted. This takes about 10 minutes, and with fruit and coffee is a wholesome meal.

Make **FRIED GRITS** when you have leftovers. Refrigerate grits in a shallow pan, slice, dip in egg, and fry brown in bacon drippings. Wonderful with crisp bacon!

Leftover potatoes may be sliced and browned in butter, or creamed potatoes may be made into little **POTATO PATTIES** the size of a biscuit, dipped in corn meal, and fried in bacon drippings. Oh, there are endless things to do if you just have a few gold mines in your ice box.

Fruits are essential for breakfast, to stir into active being a stomach which has been sleeping all night.

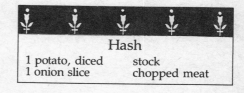

Hash

| 1 potato, diced | stock |
| 1 onion slice | chopped meat |

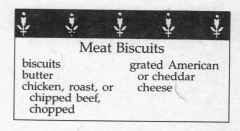

Meat Biscuits

biscuits	grated American
butter	or cheddar
chicken, roast, or	cheese
chipped beef,	
chopped	

Fried Grits

| cold grits | bacon drippings |
| 1 egg | |

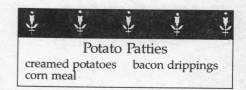

Potato Patties

| creamed potatoes | bacon drippings |
| corn meal | |

9

Try **PRUNE TOAST.** Stewed prunes are good, as well as good for you. They are delicious if seeded, mashed, and spread on hot, buttered toast.

Prune Toast	
stewed prunes	hot, buttered toast

Apples may be used as sauce, in fritters, broiled on a grill with your ham or bacon, or fried, either in rings or in quarters.

For **FRIED APPLES,** core apples, slice into ½-inch slices, and fry in bacon drippings. When done, sprinkle with powdered sugar. Or for **FRIED APPLES À LA HIGHLANDS,** quarter green apples, remove cores, and put in skillet with bacon drippings. Let brown and add a bit of water, cover and cook until tender. Serve with ham, sausage, or bacon.

Fried Apples	
apples	powdered sugar
bacon drippings	

Fried Apples à la Highlands	
green apples	water
bacon drippings	

For Sunday breakfast try **POTATO MARGE**: Peel and dice 2 Irish potatoes, fry in bacon drippings. Pour off any unused fat from pan. Over the potatoes in the hot pan, pour 4 slightly beaten eggs and fold over until all eggs are cooked. Serve this with slices of cold, raw tomato and hot toast and you've got something. You may add a little chipped beef, sausage, bacon, or diced ham to this, too. Serves 2.

Potato Marge	
2 potatoes	4 eggs, slightly beaten
bacon drippings	

Just one more word about breakfast: Look pretty. Take time to put on a fresh cotton dress or brunch coat; see that your hair is pretty. Never, never look sloppy for breakfast. That is the picture that Dick will carry all day, so see that it is a pretty picture.

And regardless of the fashionable idea of little or no breakfast, give Dick a good, substantial meal. He'll be a better husband, a more successful man, and a healthier brute if he gets into the habit of a good breakfast.

To go back for a moment to the amount of food you cook — be a generous cook! By this I do not mean for you to be extravagant or wasteful. I hate both with a passion, and your husband's success in life depends entirely upon the contents of your garbage pail. No, not these two, but be generous with

what you cook. Life is abundant and abundance is here on God's earth for you, provided you know how to use it. And how important that "how to use it" is! By that we measure the richness and fullness of life, the number of friends we have, the material possessions we acquire, the character we attain.

You've always been unselfish with yourself — giving the best that was in you to others. Now learn to share the richest part of your life by giving away part of the things you learn to make with your hands. You cannot really give away anything, because no matter what you give away you get more than you give! Think about that a minute and you'll see that it's true. Does anything else make you feel as good as that little glow that seeps into your heart when you've given away something nice? Does any cosmetic make you as pretty as the sparkle that lights up your face when you've given pleasure to someone else?

When you make something delicious — a pie, a custard, hot rolls, spaghetti — make more than you need and take a bit next door, or to the pregnant lady down the street, or call in the children playing in the yard. Share what you have and share generously. Is someone moving across the hall? Ask them to share your supper. They are probably rather tired. Share something or do something nice for somebody every day. Whether you be a Boy Scout or married lady, giving of yourself to others is the most enriching rule of life.

And so, my dear, with this little sermon —

Goodnight and Love,
Mother

Atlanta, Georgia
June 20, 1942

Dearest Selma:

I can scarcely wait to hear how you are getting along with those first breakfast recipes. Every afternoon Bella says, "Wonder what Miss Selma's giving Mr. Dick for breakfasts." I wonder too, but this War Bond drive has me flying in so many directions, I have little time to express my thoughts.

To return to your lessons in "Culinary Success" — perhaps I'd better tell you now **THE THEORY OF COOKING**. It's sort of like writing. You know that there are rules and mechanics for the pen which have to be completely mastered — and then forgotten — before one can build short stories, novels, etc. You learn these rules and patterns, study your ingredients (words and plots), and inspiration or not, you get to work to create a product.

Likewise, there are certain rules and patterns — secrets you might say — of cooking, and these must be as familiar as the hairline on your forehead before you can begin using the utensils and ingredients, which, combined with skill, will become no less than a creation. There's an art to cooking just as there's an art to writing, and the old saying that "Writing is nine-tenths perspiration and one-tenth inspiration," is equally applicable to cooking.

Cooking does take courage as well as imagination and ingenuity. Only the brave can face an expensive assortment of ingredients and calmly mix them into a masterpiece of flavor and design. Ruskin was right about cooking: "Cookery means the knowledge of Medea and of Circe and of Helen and of the Queen of Sheba. It means the knowledge of all herbs and fruits and balms and spices and all that is healing and sweet in the fields and groves and savory in meats. It means carefulness and inventiveness and willingness and readiness of appliances. It means the economy of your Grandmothers and the science

of the modern chemist; it means much testing and no wasting; it means English thoroughness and French art and Arabian hospitality; and, in fine, it means that you are to be perfectly and always, ladies — loaf givers."

So hold your head high, straighten your back, and dive in. If (and it happens in the best of kitchens) your ingredients turn into an awful flop, just toss it away — and keep quiet. The successful wives are those who hide their failures.

In most of my recipes I avoid fractions whenever possible, for the simple reason that I've hated fractions ever since the first day I was introduced to them in school, and when I see a recipe which starts off with a long list of things like this:

½ cup milk
¼ Tsp. that
¾ Tbl. of the other
½ cup flour
etc.

Well, I just have fits and go on and make something else. I haven't time nor inclination to do a mathematical problem to measure a pinch of soda. I've found that ¼ teaspoonful is the same amount you can hold on a dime, and while I do not use a dime for measurement, having measured it once, I can tell exactly how much to put in the end of a spoon. When I say a pinch I mean just that — just what you can hold between your thumb and forefinger.

I like recipes like my grandmother used:

1 pound butter
1 pound eggs
1 pound flour
1 cup milk
1 Tbl. baking powder

Now, that's my idea of how a recipe should look, but in these restricted wartime days I fear we'll have to do without the famous pound cake, and use fractions even if we do not write them out. So until you've acquired a practiced eye by actually measuring, you'd best use your measuring cups and spoons. But it won't be long before you can cook by eye as Bella and I do. When you've reached that stage, you've acquired freedom in cooking and you'll find you can improve on almost any given recipe. The main thing is to memorize all the basic recipes so thoroughly that you could almost make them in your sleep.

Taking for granted your courage and a vivid imagination, I suggest the following as **FUNDAMENTAL RECIPES** which, once having been mastered, may be dismissed from your mind.

For **BASIC WHITE SAUCE**, use 1 Tbl. butter, 1 Tbl. flour, and 1 cup milk. Melt butter in sauce pan. Add flour and rub smooth. Add milk and cook until thick, stirring constantly. Salt and pepper to taste. Warm milk slightly before adding to flour and butter. This may be varied in many ways as you will see as you progress in this streamlined course in cooking. The above recipe is for thin white sauce. For medium sauce increase butter and flour to 2 Tbl. and for thick sauce increase to 3 Tbl.

Next is **BASIC DESSERT SAUCE** — the ubiquitous little item which decides whether you are a chef or just a garden variety cook. So get it firmly in your mind and make it often. Dissolve 1 Tbl. cornstarch in ½ cup water. Mix with 1 cup sugar and ½ stick of butter. Cook until it boils five minutes. This is basic. Now you may add flavoring: 2 oz. wine, 2 oz. rum, 1 Tbl. vanilla extract, 1 Tbl. creme de cacao, etc. Makes 1 cup. Make orange or lemon sauce the same way, except instead of water you use the juice and grated rind of 2 lemons or 2 oranges.

Basic White Sauce

| 1 Tbl. butter | 1 cup milk |
| 1 Tbl flour | salt and pepper, to taste |

Basic Dessert Sauce

1 Tbl. cornstarch	½ stick of butter
½ cup water	flavoring
1 cup sugar	

Never serve a fritter, either fruit or vegetable, without a lemon or orange sauce. The sauce lifts it far above the ordinary. Daddy likes orange sauce full of raisins and nuts on anything — even meats. It is delicious on lamb. Always serve a wine, rum, or maple sauce with your bread puddings and rice puddings. You can make enough sauce for several times, as it keeps beautifully in a covered glass jar in the refrigerator.

CHOCOLATE SAUCE is fine for ice cream or pound cake. Mix 1 cup sugar, 1 tsp. cornstarch, and 1 Tbl. butter. In ¼ cup milk or cream, melt 1½ squares unsweetened chocolate and add to sugar-butter mixture. (Or add 4 Tbl. cocoa and the milk to mixture instead.) Cook over low heat until thick and then add 1 tsp. vanilla extract. Serve hot. Makes 1 cup.

To make **FOOLPROOF THREE-MINUTE HOLLANDAISE**, first separate 2 eggs. Put the yolks into the top of a small double boiler. Add the juice of 2 lemons (about 3 Tbl.) and mix well. Moisten 1 tsp. cornstarch in 2 Tbl. milk and add to egg mixture. Add 2 Tbl. butter. Cook over boiling water, but do not let water touch bottom of top pan. Stir with wire whisk until thick and creamy. Remove from hot water and add 1 tsp. salt. This may be made ahead and reheated over warm water. Makes 1 cup. The secret of this Hollandaise sauce is that the little bit of cornstarch keeps it from curdling. If too thick, add hot water or cream.

If used on fish, add 2 Tbl. grated horseradish and ¼ cup chopped capers, for **FISH HOLLANDAISE**.

For **SAUCE MARGERY**, add 1 cup of cooked shrimp and 1 cup of cooked crab meat to Fish Hollandaise, and serve on baked fish from which the skin and bones have been removed, or serve on broiled filets of fish. Delicious!

I used to make **MAYONNAISE** by the 3 and 4 gallons for the boys at the University of Georgia when big parties were afoot. They did the beating

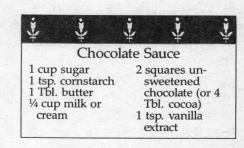

Chocolate Sauce

1 cup sugar	2 squares un-
1 tsp. cornstarch	sweetened
1 Tbl. butter	chocolate (or 4
¼ cup milk or	Tbl. cocoa)
cream	1 tsp. vanilla
	extract

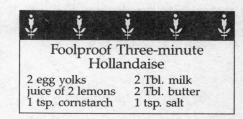

Foolproof Three-minute Hollandaise

2 egg yolks	2 Tbl. milk
juice of 2 lemons	2 Tbl. butter
1 tsp. cornstarch	1 tsp. salt

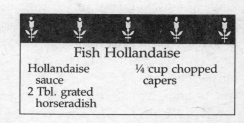

Fish Hollandaise

Hollandaise	¼ cup chopped
sauce	capers
2 Tbl. grated	
horseradish	

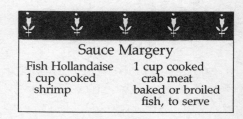

Sauce Margery

Fish Hollandaise	1 cup cooked
1 cup cooked	crab meat
shrimp	baked or broiled
	fish, to serve

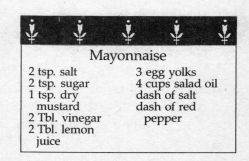

Mayonnaise

2 tsp. salt	3 egg yolks
2 tsp. sugar	4 cups salad oil
1 tsp. dry	dash of salt
mustard	dash of red
2 Tbl. vinegar	pepper
2 Tbl. lemon	
juice	

while I poured, and it was as stiff and pretty as I've ever seen. In a mixing bowl, put 2 tsp. salt, 2 tsp. sugar, and 1 tsp. dry mustard and mix together. Add 2 Tbl. vinegar and 2 Tbl. lemon juice. Mix and add yolks of 3 eggs. Beat with a wire egg beater, whisk, or electric mixer, but do not let mixture become foamy. Start adding 4 cups of salad oil a tsp. at a time. Increase to pouring in a thin stream, beating hard all the time. As soon as enough oil has been added to look smooth and slightly thick, you may hasten the process by pouring as fast as you can mix it. When it is stiff and all oil is used, beat another minute, season with a dash of salt and red pepper, and put into a glass jar to store in the ice box. Makes 1 qt.

Remember how your friends used to love the **SANDWICH MAYONNAISE**? To makes this I always add to 1 pt. mayonnaise, 2 cups grated cheddar cheese, ¼ cup finely chopped pickle, and ½ cup finely chopped capers. This keeps indefinitely and is always ready for a grand spread. Dick would like a sandwich of this when he comes in from a strenuous day of flying.

Men always think there is a special magic in a **BAKED CUSTARD** and marvel when they see one in a home. Well, I don't blame them, because so few women know how to make them. They are so easy, so nourishing, and so delicious that I want you to make them often. There are two secrets which have to be mastered or you will fail every time. The first is to get your proportions right: Measure 1 egg, and 1 level Tbl. sugar to each level cup milk and mix well. No more, no less, and try to have nice, large, fresh eggs. That's all there is to it, except a dash of vanilla and a pinch of salt. And the second secret: Set the custard cups or baking dish in a pan of water and bake. I turn on my oven after I put the custard in, setting it at about 350°. The custard should stay in about an hour to be firm and slightly brown. Always remember that any dish with eggs and milk must be cooked very slowly or those ingredients will sepa-

Sandwich Mayonnaise

1 pt. mayonnaise	¼ cup finely
2 cups grated	chopped pickle
cheddar cheese	½ cup finely
	chopped capers

Baked Custard

1 egg and 1 Tbl.	pinch of salt
sugar to every	
1 cup milk	
dash of vanilla	

rate. Do not let water in pan boil — add more if necessary. Allow to cool before serving. If you cook it in one baking dish, do not put a spoon in it until it is quite cold. One cup of milk serves 2. This is still Bec's favorite dessert.

The French people say they could live on what we waste, and I do not doubt it until I try making a French delicacy which invariably calls for every expensive item in the store. Be that as it may, the French do save everything and what's more they use everything they save. They would never be caught without a jar of meat or vegetable **STOCK** in the ice box!

When you cook roasts or meats of any sort, boil up the trimmings and bones for stock, adding an onion, carrot, and celery stalk. Always save chicken stock or the surplus liquid from vegetables, as these are excellent starters for soups and gravies.

Gravy may be made from any meats or fowl. To make **PAN GRAVY**, first remove cooked meat from pan. If there is much juice in pan, pour off into a cup. Skim off fat. Return 2 Tbl. fat to meat pan. Add 2 Tbl. flour. Stir until smooth and brown. Add juices and water to make 1½ cups. Cook until smooth and thickened. Makes 1 cup. Double to serve 4. Taste for flavor, and season with bouillon cubes or B.V. extract if flavor is weak. To thicken chicken stock without browning, mix 2 Tbl. flour in 1 cup water and strain into 1½ cups stock. Cook until thick and smooth. Season. Makes about 1 cup.

The **CANNED SOUPS** are so handy and delicious that I advise their use for the present. Try combining two varieties — it's interesting to discover how many delicious soups can be concocted by the simple expedient of two cans and a can opener. Soups may be made attractive by the addition of croutons (small squares of toast), crushed crackers, chopped parsley or watercress, or a spoonful of sour cream or

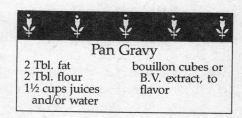

Pan Gravy

2 Tbl. fat	bouillon cubes or
2 Tbl. flour	B.V. extract, to
1½ cups juices and/or water	flavor

whipped cream. Soups make excellent starters for light or heavy meals, as they are appetizing and the hot, savory flavors start the digestive gastric juices flowing.

For **HOMEMADE CHICKEN SOUP** (just in case), the next time you stew a chicken, add an onion, a celery stalk, and a carrot to the water. Save the resulting stock and chill. When cold, remove congealed fat and add cooked rice or noodles and chopped chicken to stock for a delicious fresh soup. Season with salt and pepper and celery seeds.

BASIC CORNSTARCH PUDDING is a splendid beginning to many tempting desserts. The secrets are careful blending, much stirring, and slow heat. It is delicious with any of the dessert sauces, with whipped cream, or with crushed fruit or nuts, so use this often. Remember that *to each cup of milk you use 2 level Tbl. cornstarch and 2 Tbl. sugar.* Mix the latter two together with enough of the cold milk to soften, add 1 egg, and pour into the rest of the milk which has been heated, stirring until smooth and transparent. For 2 cups milk use 4 Tbl. cornstarch, 4 Tbl. sugar, and 1 or 2 eggs, using ½ cup cold milk and 1½ cups hot milk. Cook over a slow heat until thick, stirring constantly. Flavor with 1 tsp. almond extract, lemon extract, vanilla extract, or rum. By adding 4 Tbl. cocoa you can make it into a grand chocolate pudding! Serves 4 to 6.

GELATIN is the kitchen miracle! Use it often, not only because it combines so many ingredients into palatable dishes, but because it is rich in protein and easily digested. The thing to remember is that 1 envelope jells 1 pint of liquid or custard. But if you want to *mold*, then add an extra envelope of gelatin so that your mold won't melt if it has to stand after being unmolded.

Soften 1 envelope gelatin in ½ cup cold water, then add 1½ cups boiling water or fruit or vegetable juices (tomato juice is nice with meat salads) to dissolve it. Never boil gelatin. This is basic and makes a dessert

Homemade Chicken Soup

stock from stewed chicken, to which has been added 1 onion, 1 carrot, and 1 celery stalk	salt and pepper celery seeds
cooked rice or noodles	
chopped chicken	

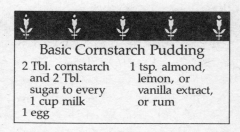

Basic Cornstarch Pudding

2 Tbl. cornstarch and 2 Tbl. sugar to every 1 cup milk	1 tsp. almond, lemon, or vanilla extract, or rum
1 egg	

base or a salad base with the addition of fruits or vegetables, but always remember to allow more gelatin if you mold.

For **LEMON GELATIN** use 1 Tbl. gelatin, ¼ cup cold water, ¾ cup boiling water, 1 cup sugar, and ¼ cup lemon juice. Soak gelatin in cold water 10 minutes. Slowly add the hot water and stir until dissolved. Add sugar and lemon juice and stir until sugar is dissolved. Strain into molds and chill.

One final fundamental recipe that you're sure to use all the time is **FRENCH DRESSING**. Because it's perfect as a marinade for vegetables or meats or for serving with a multitude of salads, make sure you always have a generous serving of this basic dressing in your ice box. To make, mix 3 parts pure olive oil or salad oil to 1 part cider vinegar. Add a few capers to this mixture, along with some of the juice. Add salt and pepper to taste, and a few dashes of Tabasco sauce and Worchestershire sauce, as needed. Refrigerate in a pretty glass bottle, and voila!

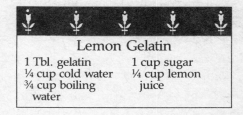

Lemon Gelatin

1 Tbl. gelatin	1 cup sugar
¼ cup cold water	¼ cup lemon
¾ cup boiling water	juice

French Dressing

3 parts pure olive oil or salad oil to 1 part cider vinegar	tabasco sauce, to taste
a few capers and juice, to taste	Worchestershire sauce, to taste
salt and pepper, to taste	

Here are a few notes which may insult your intelligence but one never knows! **EQUIVALENT MEASUREMENTS**:

3 teaspoons equal 1 tablespoon
16 tablespoons equal 1 cup
2 cups equal 1 pint
4 tablespoons flour equal 1 ounce
2 cups sugar equal 1 pound
2 tablespoons butter equal 1 ounce

These are facts of importance in a kitchen where utensils are scarce. Another bit of advice — buy the same kind of baking powder all the time because the different brands vary so much. You will soon know whether to use a generous teaspoonful or a scant one.

Here are important **COOKING TERMS**: When I

say *broil*, I mean under-the-flame cooking. *Sauté* is cooking in butter in the frying pan. *Frying* means cooking in moderate fat in the frying pan. *Deep fat frying* is cooking in fat 4 inches deep, usually in a heavy, deep boiler. *Boiling* is cooking in water in a covered skillet or sauce pan. *Roasting* is in a hot oven. *Baking* means cooking in a moderate oven.

Now, a word to the wise about **NUTRITION**: There are certain food elements essential to health and well being, not to mention beauty, and our foods must supply these unless we fill up on vitamin pills. I am a great believer in the old adage, "We are what we eat."

Lest you become befuddled with too much talk of vitamins and calories, I simply suggest that you use color as your barometer in meal planning. For instance, serve a yellow or red cocktail or soup (tomato juice, orange juice, etc.), a brown dish (meat or meat substitute), a white dish (rice or spoon bread (see page 94-95) or Irish potatoes), a green and yellow vegetable (either cooked or in salad), and a dessert or sweet. There is a meal full of calories and vitamins — all the essential minerals, fats, carbohydrates, and proteins.

See that both you and Dick drink a pint of milk a day, have your daily egg, and at least two pats of butter or margarine at each meal. Serve fruit in some form every day. And remember that whole grain cereals hold abundant life when sugar and cream are added.

Parsley and watercress are beauty aids — they put that sparkle in your eyes — one teaspoon of parsley is as good as a head of lettuce. Both of these make tempting salads.

When I say *separate* your eggs I do not mean put them on the four corners of the table! And when I say beat them I do not mean hit them with a mallet. Surely you know that separate means to crack them through the middle and hold so that the yolk remains in half the shell, while the white flows into

the bowl.

Don't use too many flowers on your table, a few interestingly arranged are much more to be desired. I have never yet forgiven a hostess whose table decoration was so high that I couldn't see or be seen by the most attractive man I ever met who sat across the table from me. Who knows what might have happened had my hostess had good taste?

GARNISHES for food are attractive, provided they are suitable and add flavor and interest. Personally, I like to use parsley, watercress, olives, radish roses, pepper rings, hard-boiled eggs, nuts, or fruit any time a platter calls for them. And they do call! Sometimes they scream out and if you don't dress them up they go to the table in a very depressed mood. The only garnish which isn't edible which I sometimes use for dinner or buffet supper platters, is camellias made from slices of turnips.

Slice turnips crosswise into ¼-inch slices. Peel each slice with a paring knife or scissors. Cut around edges to make petals. Tint these with a water color brush and red vegetable coloring, to look like camellias. Place a small one on top of a large one and hold together with piece of toothpick. These look exactly like variegated camellias and garnish salad platters and meat platters with distinction. Be sure to leave lots of the white turnip showing, just blending the colors on the edges of the petals. Leaves may be made by cutting the small pieces into long, slender shapes and coloring with green vegetable coloring.

Just one more thing tonight — **DISHWASHING**! This can be, and often is, a bugaboo even to the most experienced housekeeper. But I contend that it is all a state of mind, and I practice what I preach. After all these many years, I still like to wash dishes, and I often find my greatest freedom of mind while doing so, because while my hands are busy in hot suds, my thoughts are miles and miles away having a holiday in daydreams. This is because I have washed dishes so many times that it has become automatic

and requires no thought.

As a general rule I am not systematic but when it comes to dishwashing I'm all system: Take a huge tray to the table at the end of the meal and load it up with the dirty dishes so they all can be carried out at once. Put away your linens and leave your dining table in order. Sweep up any crumbs and straighten chairs. Now that the dining room stage is completed, we start on the kitchen.

First, collect all knives, forks, and spoons off the tray and place in a pile. Scrape all crumbs, scraps, and dough into the waste can, and wipe off greasy dishes with soft paper. Dishes with egg adhering should be soaked in cold water. Rinse milk glasses and bottles in cold water and empty tea and coffee pots. Pile all dishes of a kind neatly together.

Have dishpan half full of hot, soapy water and a rinsing pan half full of clear, hot water. Wash glasses first and dry at once, then wash silver, cups, saucers, plates, etc., taking cleanest first. Rinse and put in draining rack. Scour kitchen knives if necessary. Wash tea and coffee pots with clear hot water and dry. Wash tins and cooking utensils, scouring if necessary. Do not put boiling water on china or glass. Never leave soap in sink or dish pan.

When all are finished, empty dishpan; then empty rinsing pan into it. Dry and put up. Wash counter with soap suds and dry.

I do not object to the china and silver remaining in the draining rack until the next meal, but Bella feels it is a disgrace and always drys and puts them away when she's in charge. It does not matter so long as you do not allow soiled dishes to clutter up your kitchen. Have plenty of pretty, clean dish towels, dish cloths, and a dish mop. Take dish washing in your stride!

Knowing that you have an inquiring mind, I feel that you may be interested in what foods are and why they need to be cooked. My definition of food is: "Food is that which taken into the body yields

heat or energy and builds tissues, but does no injury."

REASONS FOR COOKING:

In vegetable foods, heat causes starch to swell and burst all walls.

Makes food more pleasing to taste.

In animal food, heat coagulates albumen and forms crust which keeps in juices.

Heat softens connective tissues which build muscle fiber and make meat tender.

Heat "dextrinizes" starch.

Heat raises the temperature of foods and aids digestion.

Heat dissolves all walls in which fat is stored and sets fat free.

Heat kills bacteria.

Lots of luck and love,
Mother

Atlanta, Georgia
July 1, 1942

Dear Selma:

So you are having fun with your kitchen! I'm not surprised, because nothing is nicer than having so well-fed a husband that he just wants to sit and purr.

How to keep the grocery bill down when he brings company home every night? I ought to know the answer to that, as I've been **ENTERTAINING** for twenty years. You know Daddy's weakness for bringing folks home, and you were a chip off the old block. The difference is that Daddy was conservative and rarely brought over two while you brought gangs in.

The secret lies in stretching your meat dish and always having on hand plenty of things from which to toss up a green salad and a quick dessert.

However, Selma, the food is second in importance to your attitude toward the guests. Folks who drop in casually that way are never quite sure of their welcome. They've probably been home with other fellows and had a cool reception from the lady of the house. So watch your welcome! It takes double enthusiasm to make "drop-ins" feel at ease, so put forth your most engaging smile and make them feel the moment they enter that you really feel honored that they have come!

There is one place in Atlanta where Daddy and I always love to go, because when the hostess sees us she invariably throws up her arms in a gesture of surprise and exclaims, "Oh! How wonderful!" I feel that of all people in the world she had rather see us, and I feel so puffed up and happy that I couldn't fail to have a wonderful time!

And another thing, never make apologies for what you have or do not have. Just be calm and charming and make your guests feel at home. Select the most comfortable chairs, have ashtrays and cigarettes nearby, offer a cocktail or a cool drink, and when conversation is normal, slip back and start supper (with no flurry). Some guests like to go to the kitchen and stand around and talk while dinner is prepared. I like this and you will too, provided your kitchen is neat and you can fix your meal with ease and grace. I know of nothing more interesting to watch than a lovely young woman, who is sure of herself and her cooking, prepare a meal. So let the boys roam around and feel at home and have simple meals.

A **STEWED HEN** is an ever-present friend because of its versatility. Simmer a hen in your big, covered boiler on top of the stove in salted water and the juice of 1 lemon. Add 1 onion, 1 carrot, and 1 celery stalk to make a good broth. Cook until tender (approx. 2 hours). Let cool in the juice. Serve in many ways. For example, for **ALMOND CHICKEN**, dice 2 cups chicken, fold into 2 cups white sauce (see pg. 14), and add ½ cup sliced almonds. Add 1 oz. white wine or sherry and serve hot on toast. Serves 6.

For **CHICKEN CHOW MEIN**, add 2 Tbl. brown Chinese gravy sauce and 2 Tbl. soy sauce to 1 cup hot chicken stock. Drop 1 package of frozen Chinese vegetables (or 1 can) in with the sauce. Heat. Thicken with 2 tsp. cornstarch dissolved in a little water. When thoroughly heated, add 2 cups diced chicken. Place 2 boxes Chinese noodles (take them out of the box!) on a platter, and pour over them the chow mein. (A can of mushrooms adds distinction.) Serves 4 to 6. Boiled shrimp, lamb, or veal is equally good fixed this way, using a beef bouillon cube in a cup of boiling water for stock.

For **CHICKEN TETRAZZINI**, chop 1 cup chicken. Cook 1 cup spaghetti in 2 cups chicken stock or water. Drain. To 1 cup white sauce (see pg. 14) or 1 can condensed mushroom soup add 1 slightly beaten egg. Mix with chicken and spaghetti.

Stewed Hen

1 hen	1 onion
salted water	1 carrot
juice of 1 lemon	1 celery stalk

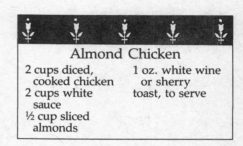

Almond Chicken

2 cups diced, cooked chicken	1 oz. white wine or sherry
2 cups white sauce	toast, to serve
½ cup sliced almonds	

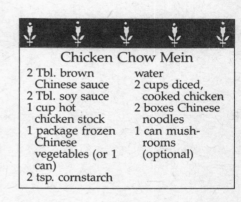

Chicken Chow Mein

2 Tbl. brown Chinese sauce	water
2 Tbl. soy sauce	2 cups diced, cooked chicken
1 cup hot chicken stock	2 boxes Chinese noodles
1 package frozen Chinese vegetables (or 1 can)	1 can mushrooms (optional)
2 tsp. cornstarch	

Chicken Tetrazzini

1 cup chopped, cooked chicken	1 egg, slightly beaten
1 cup uncooked spaghetti	salt and pepper
2 cups chicken stock or water	mashed, cooked potatoes
1 cup white sauce or	
1 can condensed mushroom soup	

Season with salt and pepper. Fill shallow baking dish or pie pan. Surround edges with mashed white potatoes and run in 400° oven to brown potatoes. Serves 2 to 4.

For **CHICKEN À LA KING**, mix 1 cup diced, cooked chicken, 1 small can of mushrooms, and 1 small jar of pimentos (chopped) in 1 cup medium white sauce (see pg. 14). Heat. Serve on toast or in timbales. Serves 2.

For **CHICKEN PIE**, line individual earthenware casseroles with strips of thin pie pastry (see pg. 55). Top with alternating layers of sliced chicken and hard-boiled egg. Put a lump of butter on top of each and cover casseroles with chicken stock or milk. Salt and pepper. Roll pie dough thin and cover each baking dish with it, fluting edges with fork. Bake in preheated 350° oven 40 minutes, or until brown. This may be made in one deep, 1½ qt. casserole to serve 4 to 6. Cooked peas and cooked carrots may also be added to stretch the dish.

For **CHICKEN CASSEROLE**, take a broiler or small fryer and cut for frying. Dip in flour and brown slightly in bacon drippings, oil, or butter. Remove to casserole. Pour 2 cups of water into pan where chicken was browned. Add a large lump of butter and heat until butter melts. Pour over chicken in casserole. Add to this 1 cup scraped baby carrots (whole), and 2 cups tiny new potatoes or potato balls. Drain 1 can Le Seur English peas and also add to casserole. Salt and pepper to taste, cover and bake 1½ hours in a 350° oven. Serves 4 to 6.

When you can find a 4-5 lb. hen, have **MARY'S CHICKEN DUMPLINGS**. Boil your hen along with 1 onion and 1 celery stalk in a large pot in plenty of salted water until tender (about 2 hours). Remove meat from bones and cut into nice-sized pieces. Remove onion and celery. Heat stock to boiling in a large vessel with cover. Have a rich biscuit dough ready (can use 3 cups Bisquick made into dough or see pg. 7) and roll as thin as pastry. Cut into 1-inch

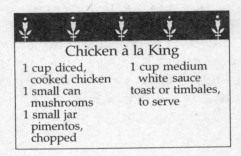

Chicken à la King

1 cup diced, cooked chicken	1 cup medium white sauce
1 small can mushrooms	toast or timbales, to serve
1 small jar pimentos, chopped	

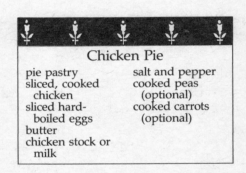

Chicken Pie

pie pastry	salt and pepper
sliced, cooked chicken	cooked peas (optional)
sliced hard-boiled eggs	cooked carrots (optional)
butter	
chicken stock or milk	

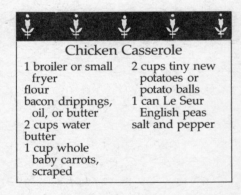

Chicken Casserole

1 broiler or small fryer	2 cups tiny new potatoes or potato balls
flour	1 can Le Seur English peas
bacon drippings, oil, or butter	salt and pepper
2 cups water	
butter	
1 cup whole baby carrots, scraped	

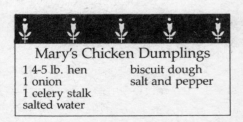

Mary's Chicken Dumplings

1 4-5 lb. hen	biscuit dough
1 onion	salt and pepper
1 celery stalk	
salted water	

wide strips. This dough should be as stiff as for a pie cover, but no stiffer. Drop strips one at a time into pot half full of boiling stock (add water if necessary), until all are in pot. Cover and cook about 20 minutes on low heat. Watch the dumplings closely to make sure that they simmer, but do not boil over or stick. When most of the stock is absorbed, drop chicken in to heat, salt and pepper to taste, and serve in soup tureen or from deep platter. Serves 6 to 8. For 2, use 1 cup biscuit dough, 1 cup chicken, and 3 cups stock. This keeps well and can be made ahead and warmed up. It's also good left over.

Try **CHICKEN FRIED RICE** the next time you have leftover chicken. Melt butter the size of an egg in frying pan. Add 1 cup uncooked rice and stir until a deep brown color. Pour over this 2 cups chicken stock, cover, and let simmer about 30 minutes or until rice is done. Don't let it burn. Add water if necessary. Serve with sliced chicken on top. Serves 2 to 4.

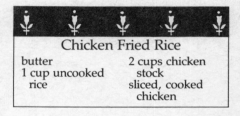

Chicken Fried Rice

butter	2 cups chicken
1 cup uncooked	stock
rice	sliced, cooked
	chicken

When the famous George Rector came to Atlanta to stage a deluxe cooking school, I had planned to attend. The first morning the great show was to open, Atlanta was frozen solid. The great elms on Peachtree were bent double with ice. Icicles two feet long hung stiffly from my front porch and glittered from every shrub. Peachtree was a solid block of ice and no street cars were running. I knew I could never get my car down the driveway and I was eight miles from the theatre where Rector, the one and only Rector was to hold forth on food.

I was ready to tear my hair but I got dressed as warmly as possible and started out at 8:30 with Daddy. We slipped and slid, picking our footing as carefully as possible, until finally a friend came chugging along in a Ford and gave us a lift into town. I had a terrible time getting home from the cooking

school, but I felt justly rewarded because I had some of the choicest recipes in the world, that were still simple enough and wholesome enough for everyday meals. I've never missed one of Rector's cooking schools since, and I'm sure he will not mind my telling you how to make one recipe I've used a thousand times, **STEAK RECTOR**. It sounds crazy, but everyone loves it.

Buy a round steak, allowing ¼ lb. per serving, and have it ground. Make it into large ¼ lb. patties. Make Hollandaise sauce (see pg. 15) — 1 recipe per 4 servings — and add 1 Tbl. grated horseradish. Sauté in butter one banana for each patty until soft throughout. Put Holland rusks in oven to heat or toast English muffins. Broil steak patties and place on hot rusks or English muffins on a platter. Cut bananas in half and lay 2 halves on top of each steak, pour Hollandaise over this, and stick a sprig of parsley on top of each. Fix 2 for each man present.

BELLA'S SMOTHERED STEAK is fine for tough meat, but you must be sure to put it on in time for it to get tender — 1 hour or more before dinner. Cut round steak (1 lb. for 4 people) into small pieces about 3 inches square. Score with knife to tenderize slightly. Dip in flour and pound in firmly to coat. Salt and pepper, and brown in very hot bacon drippings in a frying pan. When all is nicely browned, cover with water, place lid on pan, and simmer until tender. The luscious gravy is made at the same time. Serve with rice, grits, or creamed potatoes.

Down at Oxford in the good old Emory college days, Aunt Emmie was famous for (among other things) the way she cooked steaks. She did not have access to Western beef, so depended upon local meat, but I have yet to taste any more delicious steaks than hers. For **AUNT EMMIE'S STEAK**, take ½-inch slices of round or loin and cut them into 2-inch squares. With a butcher knife, score very slightly to tenderize. Melt butter in a large frying pan and then drop in the little pieces of steak. Turn

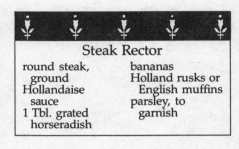

Steak Rector

round steak, ground	bananas
Hollandaise sauce	Holland rusks or English muffins
1 Tbl. grated horseradish	parsley, to garnish

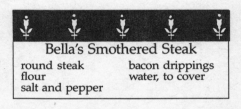

Bella's Smothered Steak

round steak	bacon drippings
flour	water, to cover
salt and pepper	

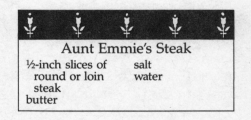

Aunt Emmie's Steak

½-inch slices of round or loin steak	salt
	water
butter	

each piece several times, and as each one becomes brown, lay it to one side in the pan until all are cooked, adding more butter as needed. Then put the steak into a deep vegetable dish and sprinkle with salt. Add water to the juice in the pan, which should be thick and brown, and when it boils up a few minutes, pour it over the steak. Nothing could be better with hot grits for supper.

For **TUNA CASSEROLE**, cook 1 cup of flat egg noodles in boiling salted water until tender. Drain. Mix a can of tuna fish with a can of undiluted condensed mushroom soup and heat. Into your small casserole put a layer of noodles and a layer of soup mixture. Repeat until full. Top with bread crumbs and heat thoroughly. Chicken is good used this way also. Potato chips may be substituted for the noodles. Serves 2 or 3.

CRAB MEAT EN CASSEROLE: Warm a can of undiluted condensed mushroom soup. Into a small casserole put a layer of crab meat (1 can or ½ lb. fresh), a layer of canned asparagus tips (1-lb. can), and a layer of soup. Repeat until casserole is full. Top with bread crumbs. Heat thoroughly at 350° about 30 minutes. Serves 2 to 4.

For **CREAMED EGGS**, hardboil 6 eggs. Make 2 cups rich, medium-thick white sauce (see pg. 14). Slice eggs and a few stuffed olives into sauce. Serve on toast or Holland rusks. Grated cheese may be added to top. Serves 4 to 6.

For **SPANISH OMELETTE**, make a sauce by combining 1 no. 2 can tomatoes, chopped, (including liquid) with 1 cup chopped celery and put on to boil with ½ cup chopped onion, 1 chopped bell pepper, and a pinch of salt. Cook until vegetables are tender and thicken with 1 Tbl. flour rubbed smooth in ¼ cup cold water. Now scramble 4 eggs as I have suggested (see pg. 4-5), leaving the eggs folded a few minutes to brown on one side. Put them on a platter and cover with half the heated sauce. (If you feel rich, add a can of mushrooms to the sauce.) Put the other

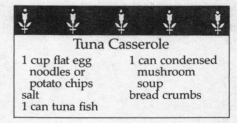

Tuna Casserole

1 cup flat egg noodles or potato chips	1 can condensed mushroom soup
salt	bread crumbs
1 can tuna fish	

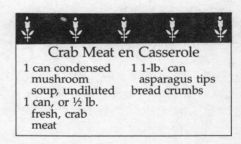

Crab Meat en Casserole

1 can condensed mushroom soup, undiluted	1 1-lb. can asparagus tips
1 can, or ½ lb. fresh, crab meat	bread crumbs

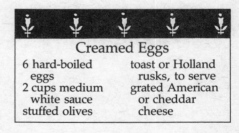

Creamed Eggs

6 hard-boiled eggs	toast or Holland rusks, to serve
2 cups medium white sauce	grated American or cheddar cheese
stuffed olives	

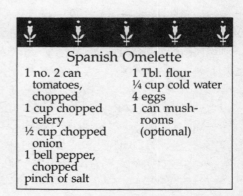

Spanish Omelette

1 no. 2 can tomatoes, chopped	1 Tbl. flour
	¼ cup cold water
1 cup chopped celery	4 eggs
½ cup chopped onion	1 can mushrooms (optional)
1 bell pepper, chopped	
pinch of salt	

half of the sauce up to use tomorrow for shrimp creole or Spanish rice. Serves 2.

To make **WILLIE MAE'S GRITS SOUFFLÉ**, use 1½ cups of leftover cooked grits, 1 cup hot milk, 2-4 Tbl. melted butter (the more the better), 2 whole eggs, and salt and pepper. Mash grits; add milk, butter, and salt and pepper. Break eggs into milk mixture and beat with egg beater or mixer until thoroughly mixed. Place in casserole dish. Bake in 350° oven until brown (about 1 hour). This is a marvelous dish for Sunday morning breakfast with a hash made from leftover chicken or lamb. But you will have to get up early (or make it ahead). It is a real company dish for luncheon or a grand filler for supper. Serves 4.

For **CREAMED SHRIMP AND PEAS**, make 2 cups rich, medium-thick white sauce (see pg. 14). Add 1 lb. boiled shrimp, cooked and cleaned, and a small can of tiny English peas. Heat and serve on toast or Holland rusks. Serves 4.

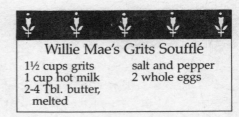

Willie Mae's Grits Soufflé

1½ cups grits	salt and pepper
1 cup hot milk	2 whole eggs
2-4 Tbl. butter, melted	

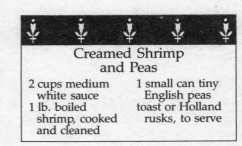

Creamed Shrimp and Peas

2 cups medium white sauce	1 small can tiny English peas
1 lb. boiled shrimp, cooked and cleaned	toast or Holland rusks, to serve

When your Cousin Stewart came home from the first World War, he happened into our house late one Sunday afternoon. Of course I insisted that he stay for supper, at the same time wondering wildly what on earth we'd *have* for supper! I went into the kitchen and took stock. Glory be! There was plenty of baked ham and a chocolate cake, but what could I use for a salad? There were cold green beans and new potatoes left from Sunday dinner and I hastily dumped them into my wooden salad bowl. I rinsed the beans in hot water to remove the cold fat, sliced the potatoes, found a few cold beets, a tomato, and a cucumber, and added a dash of onion. Then French dressing (see pg. 19) was generously applied, and the salad was set aside to marinate while I set the table and made hot biscuits and coffee. If I had worked a week I could not have had a more successful supper. Daddy and Stewart ate until I was

worried, and ever since that time I've had to make **BEAN SALAD** just like that many times a year. When Stewart left for World War II, I gave him a farewell dinner, and he insisted upon bean salad. So try it the next time you cook beans!

When you see Watercress, buy a bunch and serve it some way. It's reeking with vitamins and flavor, so let something else wait. For **WATERCRESS SALAD**, cut off the dry ends, wash, and drain. Heap on individual salad plates. Place a slice of tomato on top of each serving. Then mash a hard-boiled egg through a sieve over each and top off with 2 slices of crisp bacon, broken in pieces. Will he love this one! French dressing, of course (see pg. 19). Try to have liver or ham with this, though it also does something for chicken.

Here are some more good salads — try them!

I like to call this **HE-MAN SALAD**: Assemble 1 small can English peas, 1 cup American or cheddar cheese, 1 small can pimentos, and onion. Drain peas, dice cheese, cut pimentos in strips, and chop 1 tsp. of onion fine. Mix in deep bowl. Add French dressing to moisten (see pg. 19) and allow to stand at least an hour. Serve generous portions in lettuce cups. This is great with cold cuts. Serves 4 to 6.

In the good old days when boats were used to haul bananas, I made very fancy salads with them, as you will remember. But even now you can get them occasionally. Try spreading a whole banana with mayonnaise and sprinkling generously with crushed peanuts for a **BANANA SALAD**. Filling and nutritious.

Given 2 good, peeled tomatoes, you can make a hundred lovely **TOMATO SALADS**. Stuff with cottage cheese and almonds, cream cheese and nuts, cream cheese and olives, tuna fish salad, chicken salad, crab or shrimp salad, cold slaw, beets, or grated carrots. Or serve them sliced with onion rings, cucumber rings, bell pepper, cold beans, pimento, or cold potatoes. Add mayonnaise or

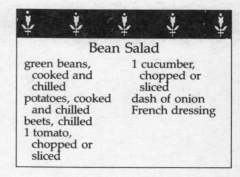

Bean Salad

green beans, cooked and chilled	1 cucumber, chopped or sliced
potatoes, cooked and chilled	dash of onion
beets, chilled	French dressing
1 tomato, chopped or sliced	

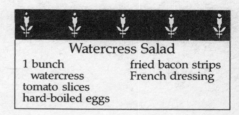

Watercress Salad

1 bunch watercress	fried bacon strips
tomato slices	French dressing
hard-boiled eggs	

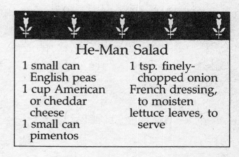

He-Man Salad

1 small can English peas	1 tsp. finely-chopped onion
1 cup American or cheddar cheese	French dressing, to moisten
1 small can pimentos	lettuce leaves, to serve

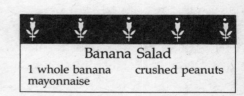

Banana Salad

1 whole banana	crushed peanuts
mayonnaise	

French dressing (see pg. 19).

One pretty way to use tomatoes is to place 3 slices on lettuce, put 2 cucumber slices on top and sprinkle chopped parsley over all. Add French dressing (see pg. 19). Keep tomatoes in your ice box always. They are an ever-present friend in time of need. And don't forget to have that bottle of French dressing cold at all times. TIP: For an easy way to peel a tomato, dip in a small pot of boiling water for 2 seconds and remove. Peel lifts off easily.

It it difficult for a couple to use a loaf of bread before some of it gets stale, so I give you this for those few dry slices you have left. Don't be embarrassed if Tom brings company home for dinner when you have this dessert.

BREAD PUDDING: Break 4 slices of bread in pieces about 1-inch square (but let them be rough breaks). Put in oven to toast, turning to get crisp all over (but brown only slightly). Melt ½ cup margarine, and ladle onto toast. Set aside to cool. For 4 slices of bread measure 2 cups milk (canned or fresh), 1 cup sugar, 2 eggs, 1 tsp. vanilla extract, and 1 tsp. lemon extract. Mix together in 1½ qt. baking dish. Add bread and soak 20 minutes. Preheat oven to 350°. Bake slowly for about 50 or 60 minutes. Serve with rum or orange sauce (see pg. 14). This is wonderful warm — but also good cold. If I leave it on the stove to cool, it is nibbled away before supper. Serves 6.

Vary this by adding raisins or currants, dropping in a few nuts, or by whipping a can of applesauce into the milk mixture before you pour it over the toasted bread. I don't know why it takes both lemon and vanilla, but it definitely does, so don't try it unless you have both.

Also good is **RICE PUDDING**: Mix 1 cup boiled rice, ½ cup sugar, 1 Tbl. cornstarch, 2 eggs, 1 tsp. vanilla extract, a pinch of salt, and 2 cups milk, and stir well. Place in baking dish, stir in a few chopped pecans or raisins, and pour 2 Tbl. melted butter over

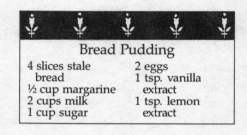

Bread Pudding

4 slices stale bread	2 eggs
½ cup margarine	1 tsp. vanilla extract
2 cups milk	1 tsp. lemon extract
1 cup sugar	

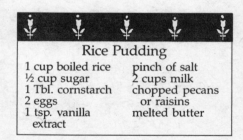

Rice Pudding

1 cup boiled rice	pinch of salt
½ cup sugar	2 cups milk
1 Tbl. cornstarch	chopped pecans or raisins
2 eggs	melted butter
1 tsp. vanilla extract	

top. Bake at 325° until firm and brown on top (about 1 hour). Serve with cream or one of the sauces: orange, lemon, maple, or rum (see pg. 14). Serves 6.

Everybody's favorite dessert is **ICE BOX PUD-DING**: Buy a box of crisp Famous chocolate wafers and ½ pint of whipping cream. Whip cream and sweeten to taste. Put the cookies together with layers of cream between. Allow about six cookies per serving. This can be made in individual servings or in a loaf and sliced. Place in refrigerator several hours before serving. This is scrumptious and so easy to make.

Now don't let all these recipes discourage you. Just try them one at a time, before company comes in, and you'll enjoy working them out.

Make popovers (see pg. 7) often. They are the delight of any meal and make a simple one seem a feast. You may want to make some sweets to go on them so here are a few easy ones you can make in no time, and if you have a few jars of these ready, you've a gold mine.

Ice Box Pudding

1 box Famous chocolate wafers	sugar, to taste
½ pint whipping cream	

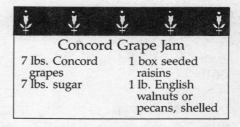

Concord Grape Jam

7 lbs. Concord grapes	1 box seeded raisins
7 lbs. sugar	1 lb. English walnuts or pecans, shelled

CONCORD GRAPE JAM: Of all the jams, Concord Grape is the best. So if you ever see a basket of Concord grapes (and you may have to wait until the war is over), make this. A basket of Concords usually weighs about 7 lbs., so use an equal amount of sugar, 1 box of seeded raisins, and 1 lb. shelled English walnuts or pecans. Wash and pulp the grapes, putting the pulp in a saucepan and the skins in a bowl. Boil pulp in 1 cup water until the seeds will fall out easily (about 30 minutes). Transfer pulp to a collander and mash — the seeds will remain in the collander. Chop the hulls, raisins, and nuts together (since you have no food chopper, use old scissors), mix this with the mashed pulp, and add water to make about 7 cups. Add the sugar next. Cook slowly, stirring often, as it burns easily, until mixture reaches the consistency of jam. Pour into hot jars,

cover with melted parrafin, and start using. This will keep several weeks, but if you want to store it away the jars must be sealed while hot. I've never been able to keep any long enough for it to spoil. It's too good to keep! Makes 6 pints.

For **WATERMELON PRESERVES**, the first step is to eat a watermelon! Then take the rind and scrape off any remaining pink part. Next, slice rind into regular pieces (about 1-inch square) and peel. Place these little pieces in a bowl of water to which has been added a tablespoon of chlorinated lime (this may be purchased at the drugstore) for every ½ gallon of water. Let this soak for 30 minutes to 1 hour. Make a syrup of 1 qt. of water and 4 cups sugar. Drop in a lemon sliced very thin. Let this come to a boil and drop in the watermelon rind, after it has been rinsed and dried on a clean towel. Add only enough watermelon to be covered with water and sugar (about 4 cups). Boil about 30 minutes. The rind should be transparent and tender. Put in jars and seal. This is as pretty as any I've ever seen and eliminates the soaking overnight in alum water. That feature always discouraged me so much that I never made it until I invented this quick way. Makes 3 or 4 pints.

To make **ORANGE MARMALADE**, wash and peel (by dividing oranges into quarters) 4 oranges. Separate pulp from peel, remove seeds, and put pulp in boiler. Slice peel in very thin strips — the thinner the prettier — add to the pulp, and measure. If you have 1 qt. of fruit, then measure in 4 cups sugar. Add to this half as much water (2 cups) and put on to cook slowly for about an hour. Stir often. It should be thick when cool, and clear as crystal. You may add a grapefruit to this or 2 lemons, but the orange flavor is so superb you don't have to do much to it. Makes 2 pints.

When you see crabapples at the curb market, buy 6 lbs. and make **SPICED CRABAPPLE PICKLES**, as they are excellent to eat, as well as to use for gar-

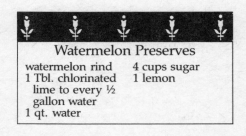

Watermelon Preserves

watermelon rind	4 cups sugar
1 Tbl. chlorinated lime to every ½ gallon water	1 lemon
1 qt. water	

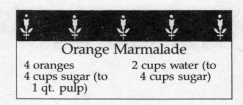

Orange Marmalade

4 oranges	2 cups water (to
4 cups sugar (to 1 qt. pulp)	4 cups sugar)

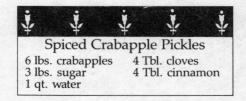

Spiced Crabapple Pickles

6 lbs. crabapples	4 Tbl. cloves
3 lbs. sugar	4 Tbl. cinnamon
1 qt. water	

nishes to meat. Wash crabapples and cut out the blossom end, leaving stems on. Stick the skins with a fork on both sides so they won't burst. Put 3 lbs. sugar and 1 qt. water on to boil. Tie 4 Tbl. cloves and 4 Tbl. cinnamon in small piece of cloth and drop into sugar and water. Boil five minutes. Put crabapples into syrup and cook until tender (about 20 minutes). Pack the apples into jars and return syrup to stove to cook until volume is reduced by half. Pour over fruit and seal. Makes 2 qts.

Write me what you'd like to have next — I'm pretty dumb about things, you know — and keep cooking! And discovering shortcuts.

All send love to both you and that fine husband.

Devotedly,
Mother

Atlanta, Georgia
July 18, 1942

Selma darling:

So you'd like to know how to prepare **VEGETA-BLES**. That, my dear, is a big order for me because, as you know, I like to *grow* vegetables, not cook them. It is the same with flowers — I love to grow them by the thousands. I never tire of digging, watering, and transplanting, but arranging them for the house is just a chore that must be done.

However, my table has always been bountifully supplied with vegetables and I think each of you children learned to enjoy all varieties. Of course none that you buy in the market ever taste quite as fresh and succulent as those just in from the garden, but just be thankful the shops have such a tempting selection, and make them taste like homegrown ones by the way you prepare them.

CORN-ON-THE-COB: Corn to be boiled on the cob should be picked fresh from the stalk in late evening after the dew is on it — it loses flavor with each hour after picking. Select the nicest ears, shuck just before dinner, wash in cold water, and drop in boiling water for 5 minutes. Overcooking will toughen it and remove all flavor. As soon as the kernels look transparent, snatch ears out of the water. I do not approve of using salted water. The salt should be applied at the table along with the sweet butter.

STEWED CORN: When corn is too tough to boil, slit 6 ears down each row, cut off kernels, and place in skillet where large lump of butter has been melted. Stir about 10 minutes. Add salt, pepper, and 2 cups (or enough to cover) of sweet milk. Cover and cook until tender, adding more milk if necessary. It should be creamy when done. This is fine also to use in boiled bell peppers, or hollowed-out tomatoes, in

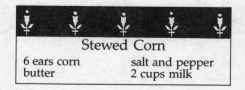

Stewed Corn	
6 ears corn	salt and pepper
butter	2 cups milk

which case, fill with corn and bake in pan with water at 350° for about 30 minutes.

BELLA'S CORN PUDDING: Grate 4 ears tender, large kernel corn. With a knife, scrape ears to remove starch. Add to kernels 2 cups sweet milk, 2 eggs, salt, 2 Tbl. sugar, and a lump of melted butter, and beat all together. Pour into buttered 1½ qt. baking dish and bake at 325° 1 hour. Serves 4 to 6. Pray that a little of this will be left over (I almost gave you a larger recipe) so you can slice it and brown it in butter for breakfast.

When Myrtle used to visit us I'd always have an extra big corn pudding, because invariably if we had it for dinner, I'd find Myrtle exploring the pantry around midnight in search of what was left. She liked it cold as well as hot. Let your pudding cool for about 15 minutes before serving it. The old problem of eggs and milk!

CORN FRITTERS: If you crave corn fritters, just cook 4 ears cut corn a few minutes in butter, and add ¼ cup milk, 1 cup flour, 1 egg, a dash of sugar, 1 tsp. baking powder and 1 tsp. salt. Drop by spoonfuls into deep, hot cooking oil. Fry until brown, and serve on individual plates (3 to a serving) with orange sauce (see pg. 14). Serves 6. Cook enough for second helpings.

I first ate these on a steamer going from Duluth to Mackinac Island. I thought them so delicious that I asked the chef for the recipe. Most cooks whip the whites of the eggs for fritters but I contend they are made better by using the whole egg. Some day, at an odd moment, you might do a little experimenting along this line and form your own opinion.

I don't blame you for wanting to have a **STEAMED CABBAGE LUNCH** like Mrs. Feeney used to have. I'd give a million for one right now!

Bella's Corn Pudding

4 ears corn	salt
2 cups milk	2 Tbl. sugar
2 eggs	melted butter

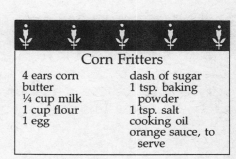

Corn Fritters

4 ears corn	dash of sugar
butter	1 tsp. baking
¼ cup milk	powder
1 cup flour	1 tsp. salt
1 egg	cooking oil
	orange sauce, to
	serve

MENU
Hot Slaw
Baked Sweet Potatoes
Steamed Cabbage
Hoecakes
Cold Iced Tea

For 6 people, buy 1 small head of cabbage and 1 large. Cut the small cabbage very fine and make of it a slaw with a hot (use pepper sauce) French dressing (see pg. 19). Set in ice box to chill.

Now wash and grease 6 sweet potatoes with butter — these should be large enough for each person to have a big one — and place in 400° oven to bake. These require an hour. Make hoecakes (see below).

Wash large cabbage and then cut into rather large slices. Cut again and again until pieces are not over 1 inch long. Have table ready, kitchen policed up, and a big iron skillet with some bacon drippings heating. Twenty minutes before potatoes are done, start cabbage cooking. Fat should not be very hot, but heated through. Start dropping cabbage in a piece at a time. Do not put in more than you can easily turn. As it cooks, keep turning it with a spatula. When all is in, cover and cook about 10-20 minutes, stirring occasionally to get it all done. Cook until just tender. Add water if necessary.

Put cabbage on platter, slit potatoes and drop into each one a pat of butter. Serve with Hoecakes, Hot Slaw, and cold iced tea, and think of Josie and me!

And here's the recipe for **HOECAKES**: Mix together 1 cup of corn meal with enough water to make a fairly thin batter. Add 1 tsp. salt, 2 Tbl. melted bacon drippings, and 1 egg. Cook in bacon drippings in hot skillet. Drop by spoonfuls like pancakes. Cook until brown and crisp. Keep warm in slow oven. Hoecakes are also wonderful with a vegetable dinner, pork dinner, chili con carne, or any fish meal. Serves 4.

Papa always said he didn't like cabbage, but when

Hot Slaw

1 small cabbage	French dressing
pepper sauce	

Baked Sweet Potatoes

6 sweet potatoes	butter

Steamed Cabbage

1 large cabbage	bacon drippings

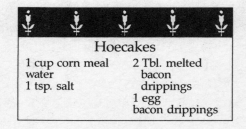

Hoecakes

1 cup corn meal	2 Tbl. melted
water	bacon
1 tsp. salt	drippings
	1 egg
	bacon drippings

Mama served **CHEESE CABBAGE** he always enjoyed it. Cut a small cabbage in quarters, steam in a little water 15 minutes, drain, place on platter with outside leaves down, and pour over each quarter a white sauce (see pg. 14) rich with cheese (2 cups white sauce and 1 cup grated cheddar cheese). Do not serve cabbage for dinner. It is only for lunch. Serves 4.

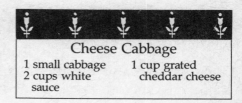

Cheese Cabbage

1 small cabbage	1 cup grated
2 cups white	cheddar cheese
sauce	

I know this will shock you, knowing that I am supposed to know better, but I confess I am a practicer of **SODA COOKING**. Now, I know by heart all the vitamin-killing reasons why I should not cook vegetables with soda. But I'd just rather not have broccoli and French beans if I cannot cook them with a pinch of soda. It's like O. Henry's "Third Ingredient" — broccoli and French beans simply could not be broccoli and French beans without soda, anymore than beef stew could be beef stew without an onion, as O. Henry proved. However, these are the only occasions upon which I fall from grace, and frankly, I'm willing to perpetrate the murder of a vitamin or two in order to have these two important vegetables look and taste just right. You are free, of course, even after this lengthy dissertation, to use your own judgement in the matter.

Personally I always select **BROCCOLI** with fairly large stems because to me the stems are more delicious than the bloom. Peel stems if tough; drop in cold water until time to cook. Do not slice them up. Make a generous bowl of Hollandaise sauce and just before dinner is ready, drop the broccoli into slowly boiling water to which has been added a pinch of soda. This should cook 10 or 12 minutes. As soon as the stems are tender, place in a colander to drain. Overcooked broccoli is worse than overcooked cabbage. Place on platter or around meat dish and pour on Hollandaise, allowing plenty of tempting green to show.

For **FRENCH BEANS**, select the tenderest, firmest snap beans available, wash, and cut into strips lengthwise. Cover with ice water to freshen. Drain and cook about 10 minutes in boiling water to which a pinch of soda has been added. If beans are tough allow them to cook a little longer but please do not overcook. Brown 1 cup mushrooms in butter and pour over beans on serving platter. These are nice to include on a platter with a squash mold and beets.

BEETS are versatile and colorful additions to any dinner. Also, beets are cheap! Fresh beets must be boiled until tender. Do not peel before cooking. Cut the stems off 2 inches from the beet, wash beets, cover with water, and boil about 1 hour. Test with fork for doneness. Drain and allow to cool. When tender from cooking, the peeling will easily slide off. Slice cooked beets, sprinkle with sugar, and pour vinegar over them. Serve cold. Or peel, sprinkle with sugar, add a little butter, and reheat to serve hot. Serve small beets whole around a vegetable platter. Use large beets stuffed.

I must tell you about the **STUFFED BEETS** dish I invented one day when I had a surplus from my garden. Boil 4 large beets as described above until tender (about 1 hour). Set aside to cool and then remove peel. Take a spoon and hollow out a large space in the beets, chopping removed pulp into bits. Combine pulp with 1 mashed banana, 6 chopped green olives, and a little mayonnaise, and stuff the beet quite full. Set in ice box to chill and serve with any meat. They make an attractive garnish for meat or vegetable platters. Serves 4. That recipe sounds utterly odious, I know, but everyone who has tasted the result begs for the recipe. So you might take a chance the next time you see large beets. Another beet stuffing with a rather piquant flavor (use very small beets for this) is cream cheese to which has been added a generous dash of prepared horseradish.

CARROTS are a delicious and wholesome vegeta-

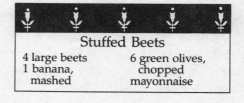

Stuffed Beets

4 large beets	6 green olives,
1 banana,	chopped
mashed	mayonnaise

ble if properly cooked. The important thing to remember is never to salt them at all. Scrape and boil in water until tender. When done add butter and a little sugar.

When large carrots appear in the winter, make **STUFFED CARROTS**. I boil them, scoop out a trench, and fill with potted meat mixed with butter, bread crumbs, and chopped onion. Brown in hot oven and serve with white sauce. Yum! Yum!

Never feel that vegetables are beneath your best efforts. A man eats what he likes, so see that he likes your vegetables.

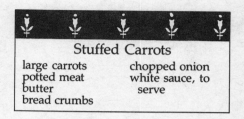

Stuffed Carrots

large carrots	chopped onion
potted meat	white sauce, to
butter	serve
bread crumbs	

I've been thinking for days of all the luscious avocados in Miami, and wanting to send you suggestions for using them. They are so wholesome, besides holding within those smooth green shells all the fragrance, sea air, and moonlight of the lush green tropics. While you are in Miami, where they are cheap and bountiful, use avocados often. Here are a few suggestions, and from these I am sure that you will be able to devise many more. By the way, avocados when peeled ahead will darken. So peel just before serving or else rub with a little lemon juice or marinate in dressing to keep pretty.

AVOCADO AND RIPE OLIVE SALAD: Buy a nice ripe but firm avocado. Cut in half. With a teaspoon, scoop out the meat in small pieces, leaving the shell whole and still firm. Mix avocado meat with ½ cup sliced ripe olives. Marinate for 1 hour with a dressing made of ½ mayonnaise and ½ chili sauce. Catsup or cocktail sauce could be substituted, but the chili sauce is better. Serve on lettuce leaf right in the shell. Very effective and very delicious. May be used as a first course, or salad, or combination.

AVOCADO AND GRAPEFRUIT SALAD: You may do the same, using seeded grapefruit sections instead of ripe olives, and French dressing (see pg. 19) in place of the mayonnaise and chili sauce. If your

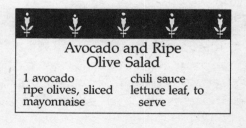

Avocado and Ripe Olive Salad

1 avocado	chili sauce
ripe olives, sliced	lettuce leaf, to
mayonnaise	serve

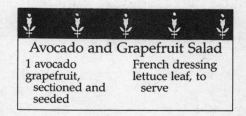

Avocado and Grapefruit Salad

1 avocado	French dressing
grapefruit,	lettuce leaf, to
sectioned and	serve
seeded	

shells are not pretty, peel and slice the avocado and serve on lettuce leaf on your prettiest salad plates. Be sure to marinate in dressing about an hour ahead to give it a good flavor.

An **AVOCADO SANDWICH** is my most favorite. Just cook 2 slices of bacon for each sandwich. Spread bread with Durkees dressing or mayonnaise. Pile on thinly sliced avocado, thin slices of onion, and bacon, and sprinkle with salt and pepper. Delicious!

While on the subject of tropical delights, we must not overlook the lobster or Florida crayfish. These are not as tender as Maine lobster but have a flavor all their own, and can be used in such an endless array of dishes that you should never hesitate to use them. The markets have them already boiled and I think you will be wise to buy those, as it requires an expert to prepare the live ones. Allow a whole lobster to a person if you serve them broiled. But in casseroles, salads, and creamed dishes, one lobster will be ample for two people. Have the butcher cut them in half for you.

For **BROILED LOBSTER**, pour melted butter over each half and run under flame to quickly brown — cooking too long makes them tough, so place them close to flame. Serve on pre-heated platter with melted butter and lemon juice in individual bowls for "dunking."

For **LOBSTER CASSEROLE**, slice 2 cold, boiled lobsters in thin slices on a layer of crushed potato chips in a casserole. Cover with 2 cups white sauce (see pg. 14) to which has been added 2 oz. of sherry. Add another layer of crushed potato chips and run into 350° oven leaving only long enough to heat through (about 20 minutes). This is excellent for luncheon with iced tea, tomato sandwiches, and lime or lemon ice.

For **LOBSTER SUNDAY NIGHT**, chop canned or fresh, cooked lobster very fine, and add finely-chopped celery and olives. Mix with mayonnaise to which has been added 1 tsp. grated horseradish and

Avocado Sandwich

2 cooked bacon slices	thinly sliced avocado
2 slices of bread	thinly sliced onion
Durkees dressing or mayonnaise	salt and pepper

Broiled Lobster

1 lobster	lemon juice
melted butter	

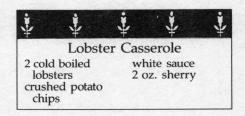

Lobster Casserole

2 cold boiled lobsters	white sauce
crushed potato chips	2 oz. sherry

Lobster Sunday Night

cooked lobster	1 tsp. grated horseradish
finely chopped celery	bread slices
finely chopped olives	butter
mayonnaise	

spread thickly on thin slices of bread. Put on a top slice and brown the sandwich in butter in the frying pan. Use a very small amount of butter, adding more if necessary. Serve these on the bridge table with hot coffee and chocolate cake and the world will look very rosy to you and you will look beautiful to him!

Here's another way to try lobster, **ASPARAGUS LOBSTER**, one of my favorites: Garnish a dessert plate with lettuce leaves. Make a mound of cooked or canned green asparagus tips on top. Slice cold boiled lobster (allow a whole one to each person or you'll be sorry) and arrange on the asparagus. Top off with mayonnaise to which 1 tsp. grated horse-radish has been added. Set in ice box to chill. This is a main dish, not a salad. Make a big dish of cold slaw and some hoecakes (see pg. 38) and that's all you'll need with it except hot coffee.

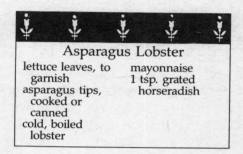

Asparagus Lobster

lettuce leaves, to garnish	mayonnaise
asparagus tips, cooked or canned	1 tsp. grated horseradish
cold, boiled lobster	

Daddy is out delivering white helmets to his air raid wardens. He left as proud and happy over his armband as MacArthur of his uniform! I'm starting First Aid tomorrow night, so I may not be able to get letters off as frequently.

Keep yours coming this way. Letters from you and Stewart highlight the hectic days. By the way, Stewart is enjoying summer school at Gordon and has been made a Corporal. Ward is getting used to the FBI, but is struggling to find a place to live in crowded Norfolk, so Sarah can join him. John is working on an airbase in Macon. He and Bec are in a motel there. His company is doing a lot of war building, so they move often. Bella and little Alice send their love with mine to both you and Dick.

Ever devotedly,
Mother

Atlanta, Georgia
August 1, 1942

Dear Dick:

Your letter was the sunshine in a busy day. It seems so strange for me to be dashing out early every morning for my AWVS [American Women's Voluntary Service] office, but there is no doubt about it — this war work is saving the lives of mothers whose children are fast being scattered to the ends of the earth. I wonder often if what we do amounts to an ant-hill, but whether we help the war or not, we help the home front by keeping all the lonely, empty-handed, middle-aged women happy and busy, and that's something. I'm glad you think our bit is helpful. I'm glad that Selma is busy, even though it does mean fewer letters for us. Busy folks are happy folks and vice versa.

Of course I'll be delighted to send the "Whys and Wherefores of a Chicken Curry Dinner," and I'm sure that Selma can have one without going into a decline as you fear. No, you don't have to wait until the correct psychological moment to spring it on Selma. I know she'd adore to have a curry dinner for as many of your friends as you care to ask.

I think Selma is like me in that she enjoys the activity of planning and preparing for a party even more than the party itself. Anticipation is more fun than realization when you are working with your hands. The children have always teased me because while I'm making a dress I have to hold it up so often to see how it is going to look — and when giving a dinner party I always have my table arranged hours beforehand so I can enjoy its beauty all to myself. Selma has always been able to get a big kick out of doing things herself, and that gift makes even the most menial tasks lose their power to become obnoxious.

There is nothing hard about curry, except cutting up the garnishes — which just takes a little time. So

plan your **CURRY SUPPER** with assurance. Invite whom you please and you'll find Selma singing in the kitchen!

The following supper will feed 8 generously: Buy 1 large fat hen, 1 10-oz. box of raisins, 1 1-oz. can of curry powder, 1 10-oz. box of currants, 1 3-oz. box of shredded coconut, 6 oz. shelled roasted peanuts, ½ lb. of pecans (or almonds), 3 bell peppers, 6 eggs, 2 large cans pimento, 1 jar Major Grey's chutney, 2 large Spanish onions, 3 or 4 carrots, 3 or 4 stalks celery, 2 pounds rice, and a large bottle of ripe olives.

Cook the hen the day before the party. Put hen in covered boiler, with enough water to cover fowl. Salt the water. Simmer until meat is ready to fall off the bone (but not to fall to pieces). This will take 2-3 hours. Remove hen from liquid and allow to cool. There should be at least 2 qts. of liquid, so add sufficient water if it has cooked too low. Cool liquid and refrigerate overnight.

Next day, remove stock from refrigerator and remove congealed fat that has risen to the top. Reheat stock to boiling in a 4- or 5-qt. pot. Add 3 or 4 Tbl. of the congealed fat and reheat. Pour a 1-oz. box of curry powder into a small bowl and mix in 3 Tbl. flour. Add enough cold water to make a smooth paste, and pour this mixture into the chicken liquid, stirring until it is the consistency of thick gravy and adding more flour if necessary. Add half the box of raisins and half the box of currants. Turn off the heat and keep covered until ready for use. The beauty about this is that it can all be fixed in the morning, leaving the afternoon free.

Pull the chicken from the bones and separate into bite-sized pieces. Set aside to be added to the curry when you start to heat it to serve. Cover and refrigerate. Now arrange the *boys* — as the garnishes are called. In India, each garnish used to be passed by a

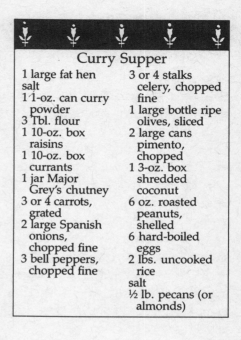

Curry Supper

1 large fat hen	3 or 4 stalks
salt	celery, chopped
1 1-oz. can curry	fine
powder	1 large bottle ripe
3 Tbl. flour	olives, sliced
1 10-oz. box	2 large cans
raisins	pimento,
1 10-oz. box	chopped
currants	1 3-oz. box
1 jar Major	shredded
Grey's chutney	coconut
3 or 4 carrots,	6 oz. roasted
grated	peanuts,
2 large Spanish	shelled
onions,	6 hard-boiled
chopped fine	eggs
3 bell peppers,	2 lbs. uncooked
chopped fine	rice
	salt
½ lb. pecans (or	
almonds)	

separate boy. So you can have 6- or 8- or 10-boy curry — whatever you prefer!

Select the largest round platter or tray Selma owns, and in the center place a small bowl filled with chutney. In small cereal or dessert bowls, arrange around this (use your eye for color and this can be beautiful) the carrots, which have been grated; the onions, chopped fine; the bell peppers, chopped fine; the celery, chopped fine; the olives, sliced; pimentos, chopped; coconut; peanuts; and last the eggs, which have been hard-boiled and pressed through a sieve. These colorful accessories are to be heaped upon the individual helpings of curry, each guest helping himself according to his likes and dislikes. Now for the rice; cook it in plenty of salted water, drain, and steam in colander until dry. (For 8 people (second helpings included), cook 3 cups rice in 8 cups salted water.)

You can make individual molds of your rice by packing it in cups and emptying onto a separate platter garnished with parsley. Serve the curry from a tureen. Or you may spread the rice out on a large platter and pour the curry over it. Or serve rice and curry separately in deep dishes. Add the pecans and chicken to curry sauce and reheat just before dishing up. Save a few nuts for the top. Also sprinkle any leftover raisins and currants on top. Hot coffee and rolls are sufficient to complete this meal but if you would like to finish up with a sweet, have Selma make one of her good desserts. Now, just to be sure you understand, I'll review.

Boil hen; remove meat from bones; thicken stock and season; cook rice; chop peppers, celery, pimentos, onions; grate carrots; slice olives; boil eggs and mash through sieve. Arrange on platter with chutney, coconut, and peanuts. Just before dinner, cook rice; heat curry with chicken and pecans added; make coffee; heat rolls.

Rowland Hill says, "Hunger is the best sauce for supper," so if you plan your party for Sunday night

be sure to have it late enough so that your guests will have worked up a new appetite since Sunday dinner.

If you do not want to serve alcoholic drinks, tomato juice is an excellent appetizer. I enclose Daddy's recipes for our favorite cocktails. Many people prefer a Scotch and soda or a highball, but priding myself upon my cooking and not wishing to impair the taste buds of my quests, I prefer offering cocktails. Your judgement on this is all you need rely on. Do not serve hors d'oeuvres before a curry supper — let the appetites roar!

To make a **MANHATTAN COCKTAIL**, use bourbon or blended whiskey, and vermouth. Mix 1 oz. vermouth to 2 of whiskey. Flavor with a dash of maraschino bitters. Mix with several lumps of ice to chill. Use a marachino cherry in glass to garnish.

For a **MARTINI COCKTAIL**, you need gin and vermouth and small cocktail olives or onions. Mix 2 oz. gin to 1 oz. vermouth. Add several lumps of ice and stir until chilled. Add olive or onion to cocktail glass. Some people prefer 1 part vermouth to 3 or 4 parts gin. It is a matter of preference, so try them different ways.

A **DAIQUIRI** is the same as a whiskey sour, with rum instead of whiskey. Use a light Cuban rum for a daiquiri and a dark rum for a Bacardi cocktail. Mix 2 oz. rum to 1 oz. lemon juice and 1 tsp. sugar. Shake with ice.

For an **ALEXANDER COCKTAIL**, use 1 oz. crème de cacao, 1 oz. gin, and 1 oz. coffee cream. Mix together in cocktail shaker with ice. One oz. of each as above makes 2 cocktails, increase to desired amount by mixing larger proportions.

An **OLD-FASHIONED COCKTAIL** is made in a glass. Place a lump of sugar in the glass and pour on a dash of angostura bitters. Mash. Add 2 lumps of ice, and a slice of orange and/or pineapple. Put in

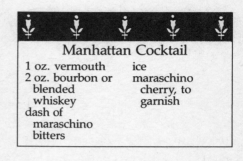

Manhattan Cocktail

1 oz. vermouth	ice
2 oz. bourbon or blended whiskey	maraschino cherry, to garnish
dash of maraschino bitters	

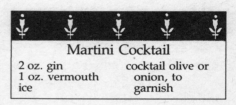

Martini Cocktail

2 oz. gin	cocktail olive or onion, to garnish
1 oz. vermouth	
ice	

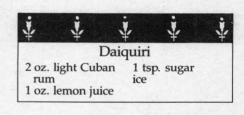

Daiquiri

2 oz. light Cuban rum	1 tsp. sugar
	ice
1 oz. lemon juice	

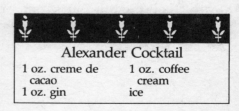

Alexander Cocktail

1 oz. creme de cacao	1 oz. coffee cream
1 oz. gin	ice

Old-Fashioned

lump of sugar	orange and/or pineapple slice
dash of angostura bitters	1½ oz. bourbon or Scotch
ice	water or soda

about 1½ oz. bourbon or Scotch, depending on personal preference. Add enough water or soda to fill glass. Stir.

WHISKEY SOUR: This is a lemon juice and whiskey proposition. Use 2 oz. whiskey to 1 oz. of lemon juice and 1 tsp. sugar. Mix in cocktail shaker with ice to dilute, and chill.

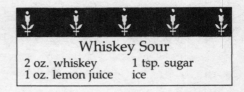

Whiskey Sour	
2 oz. whiskey	1 tsp. sugar
1 oz. lemon juice	ice

But let's talk some more about the Sunday night curry party. This supper should be as informal as possible, so I suggest having the plates stacked beside the curry platter, then as each guest serves his plate he may move on around to the other end of the table to add the colorful tidbits to his curry, picking up a hot buttered roll on the way. If your table is not large enough to seat all guests, set up a bridge table and have some of the guests gather around that. Or let them take their plates back to the living room and hold them, provided you can find enough table corners handy to hold coffee and ice water. I find that while ladies do not seem to mind juggling plates of food, men feel ill at ease and enjoy the meal more when their feet are under a table.

Zinnias ought to be in bloom now, and I know of nothing more attractive as a centerpiece for a curry supper. Use mixed colors that reflect the colors of the chopped vegetables. If you have enough gas to go to the curb market you will find quite an array of flowers. The zinnias there used to take my breath away! Be sure to get enough for the living room too. Selma knows that it is not the quantity of flowers you have but the way they are arranged that is important. She might use that cute pair of Peter Hurd figurines on her dining table with good effect.

So you see, Dick, a curry supper is really quite simple and lots of fun to prepare, especially if you are working together. And I know of nothing more

savory, more unusual in flavor, more delicious. In fact, you may feel confident of "satisfaction guaranteed."

Do write me how it turns out. My best love to Selma and to you and to quote Mr. Shakespeare — "Now good digestion wait on appetite, and health on both."

Mother

Atlanta, Georgia
August 15, 1942

Selma darling:

Your letters have been so joyous and bright that I would be foolish to spend a moment worrying over your ability to adapt yourself to new friends and new climes. Needless to say, this is a source of rejoicing here at home, for while I felt sure you would make the most of any situation, still one never knows until the situation arrives.

I am glad you have found such a congenial group of girls, whose husbands also have night flying on the same night as Dick, to spend those evenings with. Bridge is a great institution, as long as you do not become a slave to it.

I think the real secret of being happy wherever you find yourself is remembering that if you are lonely, so is the girl next door, the woman in the next booth at the beauty parlor, the fragile old lady who sells flowers on the corner, and the kindly old gentleman watering the hibiscus in the next yard. In fact, everybody's lonesome, and everybody loves the bright gaiety of youth and falls instantly under the spell of a friendly word or two.

People are the same the world over and the same characteristics which made you beloved in your hometown will draw people to you wherever Uncle Sam sees fit to send you and Dick, be it Squeedunk or New York.

    With thee goes
        Thy husband, him to follow thou are bound;
        Where he abides, think there thy native soil—

Milton must have been transplanted too!

Dick's letter of hyperbole over the curry dinner encourages me greatly. I am sending it back to you to read because it will surely send your spirits soaring

to see how proud he is of your culinary success. Only yesterday a man told me that if his wife could cook as well as she could play the piano his happiness would be supreme.

Now to turn to your questions about some cool drinks to serve at the bridge games: Start with sugar syrup and chocolate syrup, old standbys and the base for many a satisfying drink. Make them in advance and store them in jars in your ice box. They keep indefinitely and save lots of time when a rush call comes.

SUGAR SYRUP: Boil 2 cups sugar with 2 cups water for 5 minutes. Chill and store in a jar in the refrigerator to use to sweeten drinks.

CHOCOLATE SYRUP: Melt 6 squares unsweetened chocolate over hot water. Add 2 cups boiling water, 2 cups sugar, and a pinch of salt. Cook and stir 5 minutes, or until smooth. Cool. Add 1 tsp. vanilla extract. Mix. Store in jar in refrigerator. Use 2 or 3 Tbl. syrup to 1 cup milk for chocolate milk. Heat 1 tsp. butter in ½ cup syrup to make sauce for cake or ice cream.

Iced coffee, iced tea, and ice cream sodas are all delicious. A bottle of carbonated water or ginger ale, a tray of ice cream — and you can make sodas as delicious as those at your favorite soda fountain.

CHOCOLATE SODA: Mix 3 Tbl. chocolate syrup and 1 Tbl. heavy cream in tall glass. Add 2 Tbl. vanilla ice cream. Fill glass with soda water. Stir. Serves 1.

Lemonades and punches always have their attraction. I enclose a **PARTY PUNCH** that can be used for parties or for 2. Start with 3 qts. of strong hot tea, and 1 dozen lemons separated into juice and hulls. Put the lemon juice in a pitcher and put hulls in a large bowl. Pour the hot tea over hulls and let stand a few minutes. Add lemon juice and sweeten to taste. Strain to remove lemon hulls and let cool. Add 1

Sugar Syrup

2 cups sugar	2 cups water

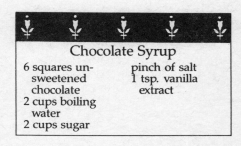

Chocolate Syrup

6 squares un-sweetened chocolate	pinch of salt
2 cups boiling water	1 tsp. vanilla extract
2 cups sugar	

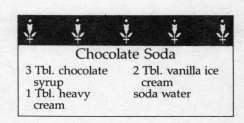

Chocolate Soda

3 Tbl. chocolate syrup	2 Tbl. vanilla ice cream
1 Tbl. heavy cream	soda water

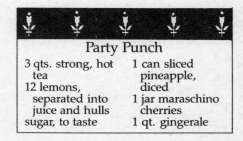

Party Punch

3 qts. strong, hot tea	1 can sliced pineapple, diced
12 lemons, separated into juice and hulls	1 jar maraschino cherries
sugar, to taste	1 qt. gingerale

small can sliced pineapple (with juice), diced, and 1 jar of maraschino cherries. Just before it is served, add 1 qt. gingerale. Serve iced. (Use ⅓ of this for 6 people.)

Don't forget to use ice cubes that make a drink more attractive and more palatable. Make your cubes different with variations.

An example is **COFFEE ICE CUBES**. Simply prepare strong coffee, allow to cool, and freeze in ice cube tray. The same applies to cooled tea. For a variation on plain ice cubes, add 1 strawberry, raspberry, or blackberry to each cube and freeze. Orange, lemon, lime, or grapefruit segments may be used in the same way. For mint ice cubes, add a sprig of mint to each cube, or try a sprig of parsley. Cider cubes are nice and you also can make peppermint cubes by flavoring water with peppermint and coloring with green vegetable coloring.

The other day the wife of an army colonel invited Cornelia and me out to have a glass of iced tea and plan her daughter's wedding. When we arrived she called us to the kitchen, apologizing because her maid was not there. We were amazed to see her juggling quart milk bottles filled with iced tea — quart bottles!

"Heavens, are you having a hundred people?" Cornelia asked.

"No, I never made tea before so I just dumped a whole box of tea in some water, and let it boil, and look how much I got."

So don't wait until Dick is a colonel to learn to make tea! *Never* boil tea, as boiling draws out the tannic acid, which is injurious.

HOT TEA: Put 1 tsp. dry tea leaves in a preheated teapot. Pour over this 6 oz. boiling water. Let steep for 3-5 minutes. Stir and strain before serving. This makes 1 cup.

ICED TEA: Use 3 cups strong, hot tea, sugar, and thin lemon slices. Fill glasses with ice cubes, pour in tea, and serve with lemon and sugar. Mint leaves as

garnish are nice. Serves 6.

For **ICED COFFEE**, use 3 cups hot coffee, cream, and sugar. Fill glasses with ice, pour in coffee, stir, and add cream and sugar to taste. Serves 6.

For **VANILLA MILK** use a glass of milk, 1 tsp. sugar, and ½ tsp. vanilla extract. Combine, shake, and serve. For **CHOCOLATE MALTED MILK**, prepare as above and add 1 Tbl. powdered malted milk and 1 Tbl. chocolate syrup.

For **ICE CREAM FLOATS**, use a tray of vanilla ice cream and 1 qt. gingerale. Put a heaping Tbl. ice cream in each glass and fill with gingerale (or Coca-Cola). Serves 6.

For **LEMONADE**, use 6 lemons, 1 qt. water, and 1 cup sugar syrup (see pg. 51). Squeeze lemons and combine juice with water and sugar syrup. Add ice to glasses and serve. Serves 6.

For **BASIC ICE CREAM**, make a boiled custard of 2 cups milk, 1 cup sugar, and 2 Tbl. cornstarch. Cook until thick. (For chocolate ice cream, add 2 squares melted unsweetened chocolate to custard.) Cool. Fold into 1 pint whipped cream and put into ice box to freeze. Add 1 cup coffee (double strength) to custard and you have coffee ice cream, or add fruit if fruit flavor is desired. Remember, you can whip cream from the top of your milk bottle by first putting into ice tray and freezing slightly.

For a **FROZEN FRUIT SALAD** use a no. 2 can of fruit salad mixture; mix with 1 cup whipped cream and ½ cup mayonnaise. Pour into tray and freeze.

For midsummer, use **CANTALOUPE SALAD**, varying it with other fruits as they become available. Use your little potato ball scoop and make balls of your cantaloupe. Then ball a peach or a piece of watermelon and cut a handful of grapes in half and remove seeds. Place these fruit balls into your little molds and pour over them enough fruit-flavored gelatin to congeal. Use a 3-oz. package of gelatin to

Vanilla Milk

1 glass of milk	½ tsp. vanilla
1 tsp. sugar	extract

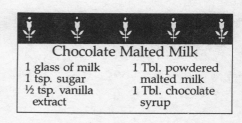

Chocolate Malted Milk

1 glass of milk	1 Tbl. powdered
1 tsp. sugar	malted milk
½ tsp. vanilla	1 Tbl. chocolate
extract	syrup

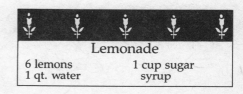

Lemonade

6 lemons	1 cup sugar
1 qt. water	syrup

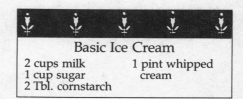

Basic Ice Cream

2 cups milk	1 pint whipped
1 cup sugar	cream
2 Tbl. cornstarch	

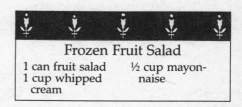

Frozen Fruit Salad

1 can fruit salad	½ cup mayon-
1 cup whipped	naise
cream	

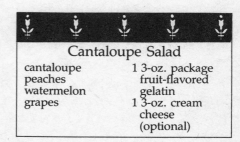

Cantaloupe Salad

cantaloupe	1 3-oz. package
peaches	fruit-flavored
watermelon	gelatin
grapes	1 3-oz. cream
	cheese
	(optional)

make 6 small molds. These are grand just plain, but if you want to be fancy, soften a 3-oz. cream cheese with the gelatin mixture and pour into the molds so it will run down between the fruits. When you turn the molds out, the fruits look as if they are resting on a mound of snow — lovely!

TUNA SALAD is a standby for every occasion. To 1 can tuna fish, add 1 cup chopped celery, 1 cup chopped apples, and ½ cup chopped pecans. Mix with mayonnaise to bind and add the juice of 1 lemon. Serve on lettuce. This is wonderful as a salad, as sandwich filling, or to stuff tomatoes or avocados. Serves 4.

For **POTATO SALAD**, use 1 medium potato per person or 1½ lbs. new potatoes for 6 people. Boil potatoes slowly in skins. Cool and peel. Slice or dice. Sprinkle with salt and dash on a little vinegar. Add diced celery, hard-boiled eggs, dill pickles, and chopped onion (if desired). Stir potato mixture with mayonnaise until coated. Salt and pepper to taste. Never serve this for dinner except when you have a light meal or cold supper. It's fine for luncheon or buffet supper.

To make **DEVILLED EGGS**, slice hard-boiled eggs in half lengthwise, scoop out yolk and mash together with a little mayonnaise, mustard, salt and pepper, and a dash of hot pepper sauce. Stuff into egg whites and sprinkle with paprika.

For **BING CHERRY SALAD**, all you need is 1 no. 2 can black Bing cherries (or 2 cups) and 1 envelope gelatin. Pit cherries. Soak gelatin in 2 Tbl. cold water. Heat juice of cherries to boiling point, pour over gelatin, and stir until dissolved. Fill individual molds, cups, or what-have-you with the cherries and pour the gelatin over them. Set to jell in ice box (about 3 hours). Turn out onto lettuce, and presto! You've got a salad. Of course, top with mayonnaise. Serves 6.

How about **TOMATOES DRIVING CLUB**? Select medium, firm tomatoes. Peel, and from the top, cut

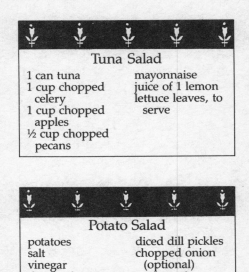

Tuna Salad

1 can tuna	mayonnaise
1 cup chopped celery	juice of 1 lemon
1 cup chopped apples	lettuce leaves, to serve
½ cup chopped pecans	

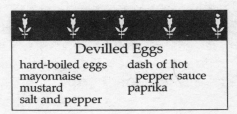

Potato Salad

potatoes	diced dill pickles
salt	chopped onion
vinegar	(optional)
diced celery	mayonnaise
diced hard-boiled eggs	

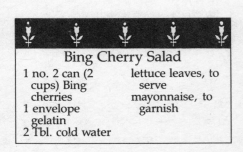

Devilled Eggs

hard-boiled eggs	dash of hot
mayonnaise	pepper sauce
mustard	paprika
salt and pepper	

Bing Cherry Salad

1 no. 2 can (2 cups) Bing cherries	lettuce leaves, to serve
1 envelope gelatin	mayonnaise, to garnish
2 Tbl. cold water	

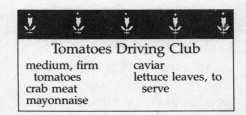

Tomatoes Driving Club

medium, firm tomatoes	caviar
crab meat	lettuce leaves, to serve
mayonnaise	

each tomato partway through into 6 wedges. Leave attached at bottom. Spread out. Fill with crab meat mixed with mayonnaise. Top off with caviar. Serve as a first course on lettuce leaf, with crackers after bridge, for lunch, or with a light supper. They are also good stuffed with cottage cheese, tuna salad, or chicken salad (see pg. 93).

This is probably a good time for you to learn to make a flaky, crisp **PIE PASTRY**, because it is basic for so many good things. I always made enough to have plenty for a pie and use what is left over for cheese straws or cinnamon sticks. These last will be nice for bridge snacks and Dick will have his apple pie!

Use 2 cups flour, 8 Tbl. shortening (or 4 shortening and 4 butter), 1 tsp. salt, and 3-6 Tbl. cold water. Put flour, shortening, and salt in a bowl and cut with knives until shortening bits are no larger than peas. Add the water gradually and mix with a fork until dough is moistened and will hold together. Roll into ball and chill, wrapped in wax paper. When ready to use, roll half the dough thin and put in pie pan. This recipe makes 2 crusts, which is enough for an apple pie and a few cheese straws or cinnamon sticks. For 1 pie crust, cut recipe in half. For cooked crusts which are to be filled, prick bottom with fork and bake in a preheated 450° oven for 10-12 minutes. Cool before filling.

For **CINNAMON STICKS**, preheat oven to 400° and roll thin the scraps of pastry left from pie crust (or use second crust). Cut into narrow strips, sprinkle with sugar and cinnamon, and bake about 15 minutes.

To make **CHEESE STRAWS**, preheat oven to 400°, roll dough about ½-inch thick, and sprinkle with grated sharp cheddar to which has been added salt and red pepper. Fold twice and roll again. Do this 3 times, then cut into strips about 5 inches in length

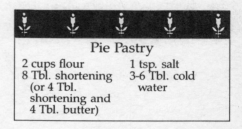

Pie Pastry

2 cups flour	1 tsp. salt
8 Tbl. shortening (or 4 Tbl. shortening and 4 Tbl. butter)	3-6 Tbl. cold water

Cinnamon Sticks

pastry scraps	cinnamon
sugar	

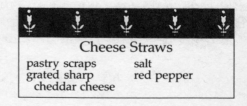

Cheese Straws

pastry scraps	salt
grated sharp cheddar cheese	red pepper

and ¼-inch wide. Twist and bake. Serve with salad.

Now, for Dick's **APPLE PIE**! Preheat oven to 450°. Line a 9-inch pie plate with pastry. Peel and core 6-8 apples. Sour ones are best. Slice and pile high on crust in pan. Mix ½ cup sugar, ½ tsp. cinnamon, and ½ tsp. vanilla extract. Sprinkle over apples. Dot with 1 Tbl. butter. Roll other half of crust thin. Cut into ½-inch strips and crisscross over top of pie. Press edges together with fork and cut off any extra dough. Bake for 10 minutes before reducing heat to 350° for an additional 40 minutes. Serves 6 to 8.

The very easiest — and some say the best — pie to make is pecan. For **SYRUP PECAN PIE**, preheat oven to 300°. Beat 3 eggs slightly. Add ½ cup sugar, ¼ tsp. salt, 1 cup light corn syrup, ½ tsp. vanilla extract, and 1 cup pecans, broken into pieces. Stir. Line a 9-inch pie plate with pastry and pour in filling. Bake 45 minutes. Chill. Serve plain or with whipped cream or ice cream.

DIVINITY: Make this divine confection and place bowls of it within easy reach while the bridge game is on. It won't help your figures, but you girls don't have to worry about that yet! (Perhaps for this the bridge girls will share some sugar — or donate a coupon or two. I know how hard it is to come by.) Boil 1½ cups white sugar, 2 tsp. light corn syrup, and ⅓ cup water. Cook to hard ball stage (syrup will make a hard ball when dripped into a cup of ice water). Beat 1 egg white stiff and pour on hot syrup gradually, beating constantly. When half the syrup is poured into egg white, return other half to stove and allow to boil 1 minute longer. Then pour this into egg white and syrup mixture. Add 1 tsp. vanilla extract and ½ cup chopped nuts. Beat until stiff. Drop by teaspoonfuls onto greased wax paper and buttered plate. Let cool and harden. Makes about 3 dozen.

To make **MARSHMALLOWS**, soak 1½ Tbl. plain gelatin in 4 Tbl. water. Separate 2 eggs and beat whites until stiff but not dry. Make a syrup of 1½

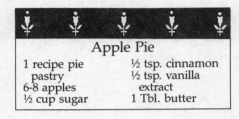

Apple Pie

1 recipe pie pastry	½ tsp. cinnamon
6-8 apples	½ tsp. vanilla extract
½ cup sugar	1 Tbl. butter

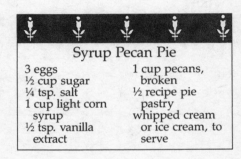

Syrup Pecan Pie

3 eggs	1 cup pecans, broken
½ cup sugar	½ recipe pie pastry
¼ tsp. salt	whipped cream or ice cream, to serve
1 cup light corn syrup	
½ tsp. vanilla extract	

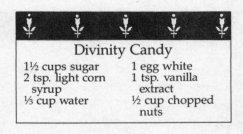

Divinity Candy

1½ cups sugar	1 egg white
2 tsp. light corn syrup	1 tsp. vanilla extract
⅓ cup water	½ cup chopped nuts

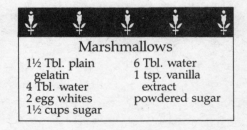

Marshmallows

1½ Tbl. plain gelatin	6 Tbl. water
4 Tbl. water	1 tsp. vanilla extract
2 egg whites	powdered sugar
1½ cups sugar	

cups sugar and 6 Tbl. water. Cook to soft ball stage (mixture forms a soft ball when dripped into a cup of cold water). Pour gelatin into hot syrup and dissolve. Pour over stiffly beaten whites, beating constantly. Flavor with 1 tsp. vanilla extract. Beat until mixture stands in peaks. Spread into a buttered 8-inch-by-8-inch pan which has been covered with powdered sugar. Cover top with powdered sugar and refrigerate until firmly set. Cut in small squares and roll all sides in powdered sugar. Squares should be about 1 inch in size. These are as frothlike as a compliment — and as pleasing. Only make divinity and marshmallows on a dry, sunny day. The humidity on a rainy day will ruin them!

For **FUDGE SQUARES**, preheat oven to 350°. Beat 2 eggs and add 1 cup sugar, ½ cup melted butter, 2 squares unsweetened chocolate (melted), 1 tsp. vanilla extract, and a dash of salt. Beat well and add ½ cup flour and 1 cup chopped pecans. Pour in greased, shallow 8-inch-by-8-inch baking pan, and bake about 25 minutes. Cut into squares while warm. Makes about 20 squares.

We mustn't forget **BROWNIES**! Preheat oven to 350°. Start with 2 squares unsweetened chocolate, ½ cup butter, 1 cup white sugar, 1 egg, 1 tsp. vanilla extract, a pinch of salt, ½ cup flour, and ½ cup chopped walnut or pecan meats. Melt chocolate over hot water using a rather large saucepan. Remove from stove and add butter. Stir until melted. Add sugar, eggs, vanilla extract, salt, flour, and nut meats. Stir to blend. Spread evenly in a buttered, 8-inch-by-8-inch, shallow pan. Bake about 20 minutes. Do not overcook! Cool 5 minutes. Cut into squares. Makes 10 or more.

For **BUTTERSCOTCH SQUARES**, preheat oven to 350°. You need ½ cup margarine, 1 cup brown sugar, ¼ tsp. salt, 1 egg, 1 cup sifted flour, 1 tsp. baking powder, 1 tsp. vanilla extract, and ½ cup broken pecan meats. Cream together margarine, sugar, and salt. Blend in beaten egg. Add flour and

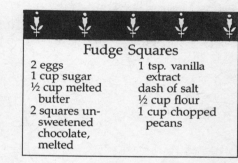

Fudge Squares

2 eggs	1 tsp. vanilla extract
1 cup sugar	dash of salt
½ cup melted butter	½ cup flour
2 squares unsweetened chocolate, melted	1 cup chopped pecans

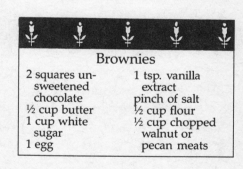

Brownies

2 squares unsweetened chocolate	1 tsp. vanilla extract
½ cup butter	pinch of salt
1 cup white sugar	½ cup flour
1 egg	½ cup chopped walnut or pecan meats

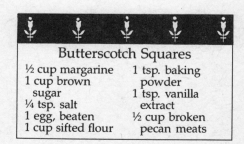

Butterscotch Squares

½ cup margarine	1 tsp. baking powder
1 cup brown sugar	1 tsp. vanilla extract
¼ tsp. salt	½ cup broken pecan meats
1 egg, beaten	
1 cup sifted flour	

baking powder sifted together. Add vanilla extract and nuts, and spread mixture in lightly greased, 8-inch-by-8-inch, shallow baking pan. Bake 25-30 minutes. While hot, cut into strips 1-inch wide and 2 inches long. Makes 20 or more.

For **CHEESE BISCUITS**, preheat oven to 350°. Cream ½ lb. butter, add ½ lb. grated sharp cheese, and cream well. Gradually add 2 cups flour, a good pinch of salt, and a dash of tabasco. Roll about ⅛-inch thick and cut with small, fancy cutter. Decorate with pecan half. Bake about 10 minutes. Makes lots!

We have never found any cupcakes to equal these velvety smooty, delicious ones of Aunt Mag's. Make the whole recipe, because they disappear like magic. And please save some for the husbands when they come by for their wives.

For **AUNT MAG'S CUPCAKES**, you need 2 cups flour, 3 tsp. baking powder, ¾ tsp. salt, 6 Tbl. butter or margarine, ⅔ cup light corn syrup, ½ cup sugar, 2 eggs (separated), ½ cup milk, and 1 tsp. vanilla extract. Preheat oven to 350°. Sift flour. Measure. Sift 3 times with baking powder and salt. Cream butter until soft. Add corn syrup, and beat until fluffy. Add half the sugar, beat until well blended. Add egg yolks, beat until light. Stir in vanilla and flour alternately with milk. Begin and end with flour. Beat egg whites until stiff and gradually beat in remaining sugar. Fold together batter and egg whites. Fill buttered and floured muffin tins halfway. Bake about 20 minutes or until cupcakes test done. Makes 2 dozen large muffins. Sprinkle with powdered sugar or ice with frosting.

Bella says I am sending too many recipes in this letter, that I'll get you "conflabergasted" — but they are all good and I could not bear to leave out a one.

Daddy says that if I can steal away from my war work, I may accept your cordial invitation and dash down for a little visit. Of course I won't mind sleep-

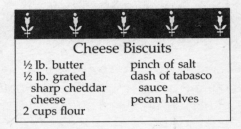

Cheese Biscuits

½ lb. butter	pinch of salt
½ lb. grated	dash of tabasco
sharp cheddar	sauce
cheese	pecan halves
2 cups flour	

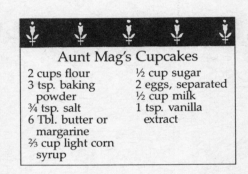

Aunt Mag's Cupcakes

2 cups flour	½ cup sugar
3 tsp. baking	2 eggs, separated
powder	½ cup milk
¾ tsp. salt	1 tsp. vanilla
6 Tbl. butter or	extract
margarine	
⅔ cup light corn	
syrup	

ing in the living room! The sofa bed sounds wonderful. Tell Dick that I shall try not to be the embodiment of all the mother-in-law jokes, and that I am very happy and thrilled over the prospect of meeting his buddies. I feel quite flattered that he wants to give me a party. Won't it be fun to get ready for one?

I'll let you know when I can come. Love to you both,

Mother

Atlanta, Georgia
September 1, 1942

Dear Selma:

I am much more disappointed than you and Dick that his transfer prevents my coming to see you while you are in Miami. But it is so grand that you are going to St. Simons. You can surely get home for a weekend or two.

I know how much you will miss your friends, how much you dislike giving up your grand apartment, which of course seems like home to you now. But I feel sure you will look upon going on as a new adventure, and continue to find life equally exciting and interesting. You married a Marine, so the fortunes of war must be yours. Of one thing I am sure — that by now you are a real Leatherneck.

But, it could be worse. As long as you stay south I shall not complain. And yet I think it would be most interesting to know other sections of the country too. Perhaps that will come later, so just thank your lucky stars you are headed toward a familiar haunt.

Don't worry because I can't be there to help you with the farewell supper party. You must have some extra special treats which you can make without me, though I shall miss the fun. This menu calls for an extra handout from Dick, as it is not the most inexpensive meal I ever planned. But for a grand finale the added expense is justified!

MENU
Martinis
Hors d'oeuvres
Roast Beef in Wine
Squash Mold
Party Fruit Salad
Hot Rolls
Exhibition Dessert
Coffee

HORS D'OEUVRES suggestions: Wrap bacon around half-size saltine crackers, broil in oven until bacon is done. Put whole pecan halves together with anchovy paste. Hollow out center of a cabbage and fill with cocktail sauce; stick shrimp or pieces of lobster on toothpicks all over sides of cabbage. Wrap ripe olive in bacon and broil. A simple cheese and cracker will even do.

To prepare **ROAST BEEF IN WINE**, buy a chuck, rump, or sirloin tip roast (about 5 or 6 lbs.). Preheat oven to 300°. Rub lightly with garlic and sear beef slightly in skillet. Place in large glass or earthenware casserole. Surround meat with carrots which have been scraped and cut into pieces, ½ lb. fresh mushrooms (rinsed) or 1 can, 1 small jar of pitted green olives (drained), 1 fresh red or green bell pepper cut into pieces, 1 bay leaf, and 1 sprig of thyme. Pour in 1 qt. red wine (or as much as casserole will easily hold) and salt and pepper to taste. Cover with a tight-fitting top and seal with a strip of dough (flour and water mixed stiff). Cook 5 hours. This smells so good cooking, you won't be able to stand it! Serves 8 to 10.

For **SQUASH MOLD**, cook 2 lbs. of squash until tender. Mash and add 1 cup cream or milk, 3 whole eggs, 3 Tbl. cornstarch, and salt and pepper. Place in buttered ring mold and cook in 350° oven about 40 minutes or until brown. Set mold aside for about 15 minutes and turn out on platter. Fill this with peas, or green beans, and have parsley potatoes, beets, etc., about sides. If you can find a pound of fresh mushrooms, broil and put them in the center with beets around edge, and you've really got something. Serves 8 to 10.

Most everything is good in and around this squash mold, but why not have tiny, whole beets in the center, and green beans heaped around the edges? If your center doesn't hold enough beets, put the rest between your piles of beans. If you use tiny new potatoes in place of beets, that's fine too. (Men will probably prefer potatoes!) Any of these make a

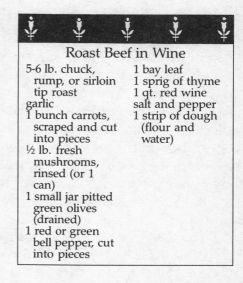

Roast Beef in Wine

5-6 lb. chuck, rump, or sirloin tip roast
garlic
1 bunch carrots, scraped and cut into pieces
½ lb. fresh mushrooms, rinsed (or 1 can)
1 small jar pitted green olives (drained)
1 red or green bell pepper, cut into pieces
1 bay leaf
1 sprig of thyme
1 qt. red wine
salt and pepper
1 strip of dough (flour and water)

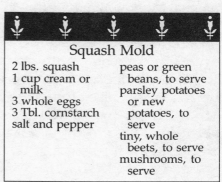

Squash Mold

2 lbs. squash
1 cup cream or milk
3 whole eggs
3 Tbl. cornstarch
salt and pepper
peas or green beans, to serve
parsley potatoes or new potatoes, to serve
tiny, whole beets, to serve
mushrooms, to serve

lovely color combination on a big round platter.

For **PARTY FRUIT SALAD**, drain a can of Bartlett pears. Mix a 3 oz. cream cheese with enough cream to soften it. Beat smooth. Put pear halves on a platter with rounded side up, spread cheese over each one. While this dries out a little, wash green grapes and slice in half. Place halves of grapes (cut side down) close together over the cheese until entire pear is covered. Let sit in ice box until serving time, then arrange platter of lettuce leaves to put them on. This looks like bunches of grapes and is quite a dressy dish.

If making this for 2, then save the other pears and try **WHOLE PEAR SALAD** the next day by putting cream cheese and nuts in the center between 2 halves. Mash the halves tightly together so they will look like a whole pear. With a match stick put a blush on one side of pear with red vegetable coloring, blending the color with your fingers. Search the great out-of-doors for an evergreen leaf, or ivy leaf perhaps, and place under pear at stem end. If you can use rose leaves stuck in the end of the pear, it is beautiful. I've even stuck a bit of privet hedge in the stem and it's fine.

Make your **EXHIBITION DESSERT** in the morning so that it will have plenty of time to chill. Start with 1 qt. of milk, the yolks of 6 eggs (put whites in a bowl and put in ice box to chill), 4 Tbl. sugar, and 1 Tbl. cornstarch. Heat milk. Beat sugar, cornstarch, and egg yolks together. Add to milk. Stir constantly over low heat until thick. Remove from stove and let cool about 20 minutes, then add 3 Tbl. crème de cacao or 3 tsp. vanilla extract.

Now the scary part! Put 1 qt. of water on to boil. Beat the egg whites until they stand up in peaks. Now (don't be frightened) with a big kitchen spoon, dip up the boiling water and pour slowly over the whites until all water has been poured through the egg whites. You see you'll need to do this in a large mixing bowl. Don't stir the whites. They will float.

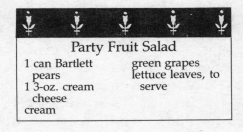

Party Fruit Salad

1 can Bartlett pears	green grapes
1 3-oz. cream cheese	lettuce leaves, to serve
cream	

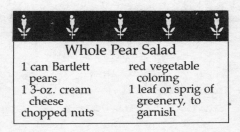

Whole Pear Salad

1 can Bartlett pears	red vegetable coloring
1 3-oz. cream cheese	1 leaf or sprig of greenery, to garnish
chopped nuts	

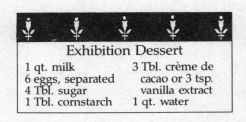

Exhibition Dessert

1 qt. milk	3 Tbl. crème de cacao or 3 tsp. vanilla extract
6 eggs, separated	
4 Tbl. sugar	
1 Tbl. cornstarch	1 qt. water

Cover the bowl about 10 minutes so the steam from the hot water can finish cooking the egg whites.

Get out your prettiest glass bowl and pour the custard in. Now (using a ladle, a spoon with holes in it, or a slotted spatula) scoop up great heaps of egg white and put on top of custard. Then dip up some custard over the egg whites. Put the last drained egg whites piled up in the center of the bowl. Leave these white. Put it in ice box. Serves 8-10.

This is heavenly and beautiful, and quite impossible looking, but you see how simple it is. The egg whites do not fall because they are cooked. Never make it the first time unless willing to repeat, because it will be demanded over and over.

For **BASIC ROLLS**, scald 2 cups milk and cool to lukewarm. Add ½ cup melted shortening or butter and 1 yeast cake softened in ½ cup lukewarm water with 1 Tbl. sugar. Sift in 1 tsp. baking powder, ½ tsp. baking soda, 2½ tsp. salt, and enough sifted flour to make a soft sponge (about 3 cups). Cover and let rise until full of gas bubbles and add enough sifted flour to make a stiff dough (2 cups or more). Knead thoroughly and refrigerate. Keep in large, greased bowl and cover tightly. Makes 4 dozen 2-inch rolls.

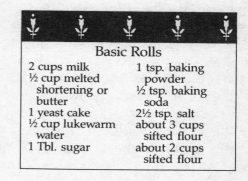

Basic Rolls

2 cups milk	1 tsp. baking powder
½ cup melted shortening or butter	½ tsp. baking soda
1 yeast cake	2½ tsp. salt
½ cup lukewarm water	about 3 cups sifted flour
1 Tbl. sugar	about 2 cups sifted flour

This dough may be used 4 or 5 days and in many ways. Allow at least 1 hour for them to rise (double in size) before baking in 400° oven for 12-15 minutes.

Use this to make **CLOVERLEAF ROLLS**. Just flour hands and roll dough into tiny balls. Put 3 balls (dipped in butter) in bottom of muffin tins. Cover, let rise, and bake.

PARKER HOUSE ROLLS are rolled ¼-inch thick on a floured board and cut with biscuit cutter. Dip ½ biscuit in melted butter, and fold over other ½ to almost cover buttered side. Press down. Cover, let rise, and bake.

Now if all this sounds complicated and terrifying, don't let it worry you. Just plan carefully so things

won't pile up on you at the last minute. Do all your shopping the day before. Make your rolls the afternoon or the night before.

First thing on the morning of the party, after your apartment is in apple-pie order, string and wash the beans, scrape the carrots, wash the beets and squash, and make your salad. Put squash and beets on to cook while you make your dessert. When done, peel the beets and store in the refrigerator. Mix up the squash mold and set aside. Now your dinner is practically ready. Set the table, arrange the flowers, and rest awhile, but watch the clock.

Seven and a half hours before you plan to serve dinner, get your roast ready for the oven and exactly five and a half hours before (by the clock) pop it into the oven. Now make your hors d'oeuvres, and get yourself beautiful. If your guests are invited for 7:00 and you plan to eat at 8:00, prepare your rolls and put out to rise about 6:30. (Make cloverleaf rolls — they don't mess up the kitchen!) Just before your guests arrive, put the beans on in boiling water. Put the squash mold in the oven, arrange your hors d'oeuvres, and mix your cocktails.

At about 7:30, when the door bell has pealed in the last guest and everything is going nicely, put your rolls in the oven. At 7:45, start to arrange the lovely grape salad on lettuce leaves. Unmold the squash ring and arrange beets in center and beans around sides. Garnish with radish roses. Ask one of the girls to help at this stage, and let her carry in the platters and pour the water, while you put the roast on a dish.

The rolls should be brown by now and the coffee perking, so call in the folks and let them start serving their plates. Let Dick carve and serve the roast, and the helpful friend serve the vegetables. Each guest can manage his own salad, while you are free to keep an eye on everything and enjoy the expressions of delight as your hungry guests exclaim over your handiwork.

Dick will be as proud as Lucifer and you may sit back and relax and enjoy your guests until time to serve coffee and dessert.

We've all been in a perfect stew getting Stewart ready to go back to Gordon. He's outgrown his uniforms completely, now being six feet tall. Can you imagine that? I wish I could keep him seventeen but I know that eighteenth birthday will be here before I know it. He tried to enlist in the Marines last week but they told him to go back to school until he's eighteen.

Good night and I do hope the party's a success.

All love,
Mother

P.S. After reading this letter over I think you'd better take them all out to dinner! Good luck!

Atlanta, Georgia
September 5, 1942

Selma darling:

I was so thankful when I received Mary's wire saying she had been able to find you a tiny house right on the water at St. Simons. It is on East beach near the big house we occupied the summer before the war, and so I think you will feel quite at home.

Since the house is furnished, I agree with Dick that you had better send your wedding gifts home for storage and take only essentials. Pack your casserole, molds, small kitchen utensils, coffee pot, etc., and take these in the car. Be sure to pack carefully your accessory shelf, as it is too valuable to abandon, and you will need it more than ever when you start making some of your favorite coastal recipes.

Daddy, Alice, and I enjoyed every word about your "grand finale" party. I'm so glad the expense and the effort expended were well worthwhile. After managing a dinner like that, you need not hesitate on the most elaborate dishes.

How I envy you and Dick six weeks on the Island! What is Dick to do there? Daddy and I both hope to get in a weekend with you but we are both so snowed under here that you must not set your heart on it. I shall be happy just picturing you crabbing and fishing. Tell Dick to take his reels, for the rivers abound in fish just waiting to be caught. Bass, whiting, croaker, mullet, and drum are in the rivers, while from the ocean come sunfish, mackerel, flounder, red snapper, and trout.

The tradition of southern hospitality originated in the coastal sections of Georgia. Since Oglethorpe built his settlement around the fort at Frederica in 1736, on through the era of the wealthy rice planters, from the Sea Island cotton kings, on down to the pleasure resort of today, gracious living has characterized coastal life.

Marsh hens are plentiful over the marshes so tell Dick to take a gun and get at least one quota. They are a rare treat. Game abounds, but that is for the real hunter with time on his hands.

You will probably find a great many of your friends on the Island, so be prepared to have some fun. And be glad crab and shrimp are not rationed.

To catch **CRAB**, tie a piece of red scrap meat (the butcher will sell you a hunk for a dime), chicken backs, or fish heads securely in the bottom of the crab basket. Set the basket down into the shallow water on an outgoing tide (low tide is best), and let it remain about five minutes. Pull out of the water with the cord, closing sides quickly, and if you have a crab in your basket, pull him up and empty him into your big basket. Drop basket again and repeat the process until you have all the crab you need. Sometimes you catch three and four at a time. Since you always left home when Bella and I were cooking them at St. Simons, I know you are in complete ignorance as to how to proceed.

Have a large vessel nearly full of boiling water, heavily salted. Drop in crab and boil hard for about 10 minutes. Dump in sink and let cool (you may run cool water over them to hurry the process). Break off big claws and put in bowl; break off smaller claws and throw away. Open crab by pulling apart at the front end. Pull off the "dead soldiers" (feathery-looking things on either side of body), remove all fat and insides, and hold under faucet water to wash. Now you should have only the body shells, with white meat left. Clean these nicely then break in half and let all water drain out. To get the white meat out, take a sharp knife and cut off the elbows where the legs were and the meat will come out easily with a little picking.

I prefer to eat the meat of both claw and body right from the shell, but if you want to make crab dishes,

you'll have to sit down and pick out the meat. It will take a dozen crabs for 2 to 4 people. Don't let the trouble keep you from enjoying the most delectable of all seafoods.

For **CRAB SALAD**, combine chopped celery, mayonnaise, chopped hard-boiled eggs, grated horseradish, and capers. Toss with cooked crab meat and serve generous portions. This is equally good with cooked shrimp or lobster meat.

To prepare **CRAB NEWBERG**, pick out 2 cups cooked white crab meat. Make 2 cups thick, white sauce (see pg. 14), and add 2 Tbl. grated Parmesan cheese, 2 Tbl. sherry, and 1 pimento, chopped. Mix in the crab meat, allow to heat through, and serve on toast. Serves 4.

For **BAKED CRABS**, mix 2 cups meat with 1 cup milk and enough cracker crumbs to thicken. Season to taste with a dash of red pepper, tabasco sauce, chopped onion, 2 tsp. lemon juice, or any preferred seasoning. Wash shells and put mixture into them. Place in hot oven to brown.

While I'm thinking about it, here's that **CHEESE SOUFFLÉ** recipe you asked for. You'll remember that French soufflés are very light and high. But I have found that most men prefer more flavor and less fluff. Therefore, I recommend this recipe. It is rich and very cheesy — a real he-man dish. Toss a green salad to go along and the two of you will eat this all up in one meal. Use 2 Tbl. butter, 3 Tbl. flour, ½ cup scalded milk, ½ tsp. salt, a speck of red pepper, 3 cups grated sharp cheddar cheese, and 3 eggs (separated). Preheat oven to 325°. Melt butter in top of double boiler and add flour. When mixed, add salt and pepper and milk. Stir. Add cheese and make a smooth paste, stirring constantly. Remove from stove. Cool a little. Add well beaten egg yolks. Cool a little longer and fold in stiffly beaten egg whites. Bake in buttered and floured custard cups in hot water or in a 1½ qt. casserole dish. Cook about 30 minutes or more. Serve at once! You may substitute

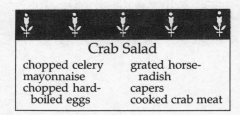

Crab Salad

chopped celery	grated horse-radish
mayonnaise	
chopped hard-boiled eggs	capers
	cooked crab meat

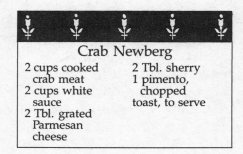

Crab Newberg

2 cups cooked crab meat	2 Tbl. sherry
2 cups white sauce	1 pimento, chopped
2 Tbl. grated Parmesan cheese	toast, to serve

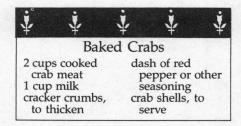

Baked Crabs

2 cups cooked crab meat	dash of red pepper or other seasoning
1 cup milk	
cracker crumbs, to thicken	crab shells, to serve

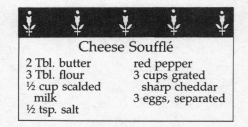

Cheese Soufflé

2 Tbl. butter	red pepper
3 Tbl. flour	3 cups grated sharp cheddar
½ cup scalded milk	
½ tsp. salt	3 eggs, separated

½ cup finely chopped vegetables or ham for 1 cup of the cheese for a heartier dish.

I believe every hostess on the Island has a different way of cooking **MARSH HEN**. I've tried most of them, ruining the first ones Daddy shot. We decided we didn't like to eat marsh hen. Then Bella and I worked out our own method and they're simply beyond words.

Dress them as you would a quail, being careful not to break the skin as you pull off feathers. Split down the back, pile into a pan of water to which a tsp. of soda has been added, and let soak half an hour. Drain, dry, dip in flour, and fry in fairly deep cooking oil until nicely browned. Keep them spread out flat so the breast is all puffed up. I hope Dick gets to go shooting while you are stationed there, because marsh hens are a real treat. Wild rice should go with them, as they have a gamey flavor.

This next is another of my "inventions" as Alice calls them. For **SQUASH FRITTERS À LA ME**, take tiny baby squash, slice longways into 4 slices. Dip in batter (1 egg, 4 Tbl. flour, and a little milk) and fry in bacon drippings. Really, you can't imagine the nice, crisp flavor.

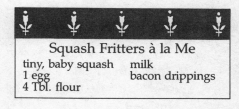

Squash Fritters à la Me

tiny, baby squash	milk
1 egg	bacon drippings
4 Tbl. flour	

If you want an easy, delicious dessert, try **FROZEN BLACK BING CHERRIES**. Place the contents of a no. 2 can of black Bing cherries (which have been pitted) in the freezing tray and freeze. When ready to serve, whip ½ pt. of cream and flavor with sherry, brandy, or even bourbon. Unmold your cherries and cover or surround with whipped cream. It makes a prettier dish to save a few cherries to garnish the whipped cream. Serves 4.

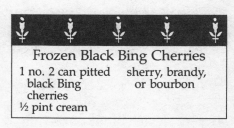

Frozen Black Bing Cherries

1 no. 2 can pitted black Bing cherries	sherry, brandy, or bourbon
½ pint cream	

For **ARTICHOKE AND ANCHOVY SALAD**, place crisp lettuce leaves on salad plates. Place a dash of anchovy paste or a whole anchovy in the heart of a canned artichoke. Place several of these on each plate of lettuce and serve with French dressing (see pg. 19). Wonderful for the first course at a luncheon.

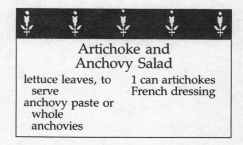

Artichoke and Anchovy Salad

lettuce leaves, to serve	1 can artichokes
anchovy paste or whole anchovies	French dressing

Serve **TOMATOES STUFFED WITH CHEESE AND CUCUMBER** when you have a skimpy dinner. Select 2 large, firm tomatoes. Wash and peel. Mix 1 3-oz. package of cream cheese with cream or mayonnaise until it reaches the consistency of ice cream. Chop 1 cucumber into small pieces and add to cheese mixture. From the top, cut each tomato partway through into 6 wedges. Leave attached at bottom. Spread out. Fill to overflowing with cheese and cucumber. Serve on watercress or lettuce and garnish with parsley. Grand for a hot summer night!

For **SCALLOPED POTATOES**: Slice 6 Irish potatoes in thin slices and parboil 10 minutes in salted water. Drain, and place in a baking dish. Pour 1 cup medium white sauce over all, cover with 2 cups bread crumbs, dot with butter, and bake until brown (about 30 minutes) at 350°.

OLD-FASHIONED GINGERBREAD is a good dessert on a cold winter's day. Assemble 2 cups flour, ½ tsp. salt, 1 tsp. soda, 1 Tbl. ginger, 12 Tbl. molasses, ½ cup buttermilk, 1 egg, and 2 Tbl. melted butter. Preheat oven to 350°. Mix dry ingredients, then add molasses, buttermilk, beaten egg, and melted butter. Bake 20 minutes in a bright 9-inch-by-9-inch-by-2-inch pan, as a dark mixture burns easily. Serves 8.

Here are 2 good chocolate recipes. **CHOCOLATE PIE**: Bake a pie shell (see pg. 55). For filling, use 2 cups milk, 4 Tbl. sugar, 2 eggs, 4 Tbl. cornstarch, 4 Tbl. cocoa, a speck of salt, and 1 tsp. vanilla extract. Cook in double boiler until thick. Fill baked shell. Beat until stiff 2 egg whites, 1 Tbl. powdered sugar, and 1 tsp. vanilla extract, and put this meringue on top. Bake 10-15 minutes at 325° to brown lightly. Serves 8.

For **CHOCOLATE SOUFFLÉ**, use 2 squares unsweetened chocolate, 1 cup milk, 4 eggs, ⅓ cup sugar, and 3 Tbl. flour. Preheat oven to 325°. Melt

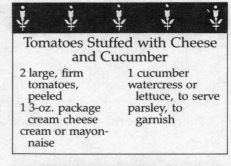

Tomatoes Stuffed with Cheese and Cucumber

2 large, firm tomatoes, peeled	1 cucumber watercress or lettuce, to serve
1 3-oz. package cream cheese cream or mayonnaise	parsley, to garnish

Scalloped Potatoes

6 potatoes salt	2 cups bread crumbs butter
1 cup medium white sauce	

Old-Fashioned Gingerbread

2 cups flour	12 Tbl. molasses
½ tsp. salt	½ cup buttermilk
1 tsp. soda	2 Tbl. butter, melted
1 Tbl. ginger	1 egg

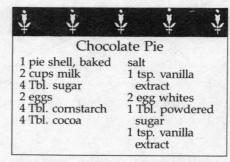

Chocolate Pie

1 pie shell, baked	salt
2 cups milk	1 tsp. vanilla extract
4 Tbl. sugar	2 egg whites
2 eggs	1 Tbl. powdered sugar
4 Tbl. cornstarch	1 tsp. vanilla extract
4 Tbl. cocoa	

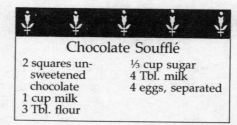

Chocolate Soufflé

2 squares unsweetened chocolate	⅓ cup sugar
	4 Tbl. milk
1 cup milk	4 eggs, separated
3 Tbl. flour	

chocolate; add milk. When well mixed, add flour and sugar moistened with 4 Tbl. cold milk. Cook in a double boiler until thick. Remove from heat. Then add beaten yolks, stirring all the time, but do not put back over heat. Allow this to cool. Fold in stiffly beaten egg whites, put in greased custard cups, and place in a pan of hot water. Bake about 30 minutes, keeping water below boiling point. Serves 4.

For **MYRTLE'S DATE NUT BREAD**: Prepare 1 cup pitted and chopped dates, 1 cup chopped nuts, 1 cup brown sugar, 1 cup boiling water, 2¼ cups flour, 1 egg, 1 tsp. soda, 1 tsp. salt, 2 Tbl. butter or margarine (not melted), and 1 tsp. baking powder. Preheat oven to 350°. Put dates, sugar, and butter into a bowl. Over this pour the boiling water and let cool a little. Sift salt, soda, and baking powder with flour; mix in nuts while dry, then mix into first mixture. Add beaten egg. Bake in loaf pan about 30 minutes.

Everybody likes **SWEET POTATO PUDDING**! Peel and grate 2 medium raw sweet potatoes. Add 2 cups milk, 1 tsp. cinnamon, 4 Tbl. sugar, 1 tsp. vanilla extract, and 1 egg. Place in baking dish and cook at 300° about 1 hour. Place marshmallows (try and get them or make your own (see pg. 56-57)) on top, and return to oven to brown.

For **SWEET POTATO BALLS**, boil and mash 2 cups sweet potato. Add 2 eggs, 2 Tbl. sugar, and 1 cup chopped black walnuts or pecans. Roll into balls. Put in ice box to cool. When ready to cook, roll in egg and then in corn meal and fry in deep cooking oil until brown. Serves 6.

STUFFED ONIONS: Sounds horrible, doesn't it? Well, don't be fooled, because you've eaten them many times and *he* will be delighted with them some cold winter night when the frost is on the pumpkin. Select 2 large white onions. Boil in salted water until tender. Remove small center and fill with a dressing of 1 Tbl. bread crumbs, 1 Tbl. grated cheese, 1 Tbl. butter, and salt and pepper. Brown in 350° oven. I've been standing in line to get onions. Hope you have

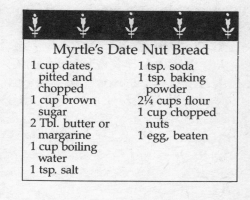

Myrtle's Date Nut Bread

1 cup dates, pitted and chopped	1 tsp. soda
	1 tsp. baking powder
1 cup brown sugar	2¼ cups flour
2 Tbl. butter or margarine	1 cup chopped nuts
1 cup boiling water	1 egg, beaten
1 tsp. salt	

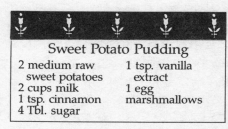

Sweet Potato Pudding

2 medium raw sweet potatoes	1 tsp. vanilla extract
2 cups milk	1 egg
1 tsp. cinnamon	marshmallows
4 Tbl. sugar	

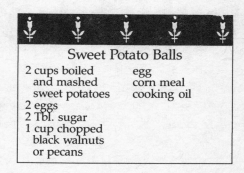

Sweet Potato Balls

2 cups boiled and mashed sweet potatoes	egg
	corn meal
2 eggs	cooking oil
2 Tbl. sugar	
1 cup chopped black walnuts or pecans	

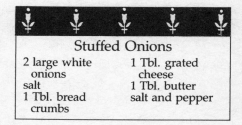

Stuffed Onions

2 large white onions	1 Tbl. grated cheese
salt	1 Tbl. butter
1 Tbl. bread crumbs	salt and pepper

better luck. The army must get most of them.

Try **SAUTÉED PEPPERS** when you are hard put for a green vegetable. Cut 2 bell peppers into 4 pieces. Boil 10 minutes, drain, and cover with butter. Or fry 2 pieces of bacon and simmer pepper slices in the fat. Peppers are a wonderful vitamin source, so don't feel that you can only use them stuffed.

For **BELLA'S BANANA PIE**: Make a **BOILED CUSTARD** of 2 cups milk, 4 egg yolks, 4 Tbl. sugar, 1 tsp. vanilla extract, and a pinch of salt. Stir over medium heat until thickened. Remove from stove and chill. Bake a pie crust (see pg. 55) and set in ice box to get cold. When chilled, fill ⅔ full of sliced bananas. Pour over this the ice cold custard. Make a meringue of the egg whites by adding 4 Tbl. sugar and beating until stiff. Pile in drifts on pie and bake in 500° oven 5 minutes (or long enough to brown). Be careful not to burn! We always put this back in the ice box until time to cut. It is simply wonderful and everybody wonders how you can have a ice cold, brown, meringue pie! Serves 6 to 8. Use the same boiled custard to make **TIPSY SQUIRE**. Line a pretty glass bowl with lady fingers or leftover cake slices which have been dipped in sherry. Pour over these the boiled custard. Chill. Serve with whipped cream.

For **SOUTHERN CHICKEN CASSEROLE**: Use a fat, young hen and cut up like a fryer (or use a large fryer). Salt. Brown *without* flour in 2 sticks butter or margarine. Remove to deep casserole with 3 or 4 cloves, and 2 bay leaves. Make a gravy out of the butter in frying pan by adding 3 Tbl. flour and 1½ cups water, and stirring until thickened. Pour over the chicken. Cover, and let cook in 350° oven or on top of stove 1 hour or until tender. Serves 6.

FRUIT COBBLER is nice. Make a biscuit dough (see pg. 7) and roll thin. Line a deep baking dish with the dough. Fill pan with alternate layers of any sliced fruit or berries, sprinkled with sugar and dotted with butter, and small strips of dough. Cover

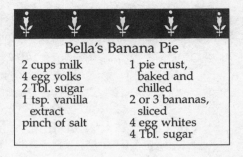

Bella's Banana Pie

2 cups milk	1 pie crust,
4 egg yolks	baked and
2 Tbl. sugar	chilled
1 tsp. vanilla	2 or 3 bananas,
extract	sliced
pinch of salt	4 egg whites
	4 Tbl. sugar

Boiled Custard

2 cups milk	1 tsp. vanilla
4 egg yolks	extract
4 Tbl. sugar	pinch of salt

Tipsy Squire

lady fingers or	boiled custard
leftover cake	whipped cream,
sherry	to serve

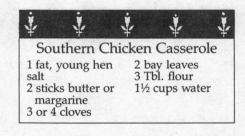

Southern Chicken Casserole

1 fat, young hen	2 bay leaves
salt	3 Tbl. flour
2 sticks butter or	1½ cups water
margarine	
3 or 4 cloves	

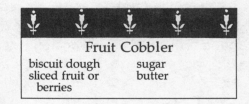

Fruit Cobbler

biscuit dough	sugar
sliced fruit or	butter
berries	

over with a crust of dough and flute edges with fork. Prick with fork. Put in 350° oven to bake for 45 minutes.

For **SPANISH PORK CHOPS**: Brown nice pork chops on top of stove in frying pan. Sprinkle with salt and pepper. Remove to a baking dish or casserole. Cover each chop with a slice of onion and a spoonful of canned tomatoes. Make a gravy in the frying pan by adding water, 2 Tbl. flour, and 2 Tbl. butter, and add the rest of the canned tomatoes to it. Pour over chops, cover, and bake at 350° about 2 hours.

This batch of recipes should keep you busy and happy for days.

Spanish Pork Chops	
pork chops	water
salt and pepper	2 Tbl. flour
onion slices	2 Tbl. butter
1 can tomatoes	

The war news is most depressing but I feel confident that when our mammoth supplies start rolling in earnest, backed up by our millions of fine soldiers, sailors, and Marines, the tide will turn. It terrifies me to think of the enemy U-boats right off St. Simons. Be careful of your lights, darling. One little gleam at night might silhouette one of our boats. Are your blackout shades sufficient or do you have to sit in the dark?

All love,
Mother

Atlanta, Georgia
September 15, 1942

Selma darling:

Thanks for your many letters. Sometimes I'm sorry I've become so involved in war work, because it is so hard to write to my own family as often as I'd like.

What fun to dance again on the moonlit patio of The Cloister. To me that setting is romantic beyond words, and it must have been doubly glamorous with the array of white dress uniforms. You must have looked lovely with pink oleanders in your hair.

How lucky that the back porch produced a crab basket. Catch them often and you'll save enough money and ration points to treat Dick to a thick slice of ham before long. Ham is always welcome after an orgy of seafood.

I'm including some **SHRIMP** recipes, because you can get such quantities right off the shrimp boats at the pier — and so very cheaply. Of course, you know shrimp can simply be boiled and then used in a variety of ways. To cook, drop in boiling, salted water. Return to boil. Cook 2 minutes. Drain and cool. Peel and remove veins as suggested by recipe. Daddy says to send you "Shrimp and Onions," Bella offers "Fried Green Shrimp," and little Alice says "Shrimp Chowder." So I'll include all these plus a couple more and you can try them out at your leisure.

Try **BEC'S MARINATED SHRIMP**: Boil and peel 3 lbs. shrimp. Remove veins. Slice and separate 3 medium onions into rings. Mix onions and shrimp. Pour over this mixture 1 cup salad oil, ⅓ cup lemon juice, and 1 Tbl. Worchestershire sauce. Salt and pepper and add 2 oz. crumbled bleu cheese. Stir together. Marinate at least 2 hours or let stand overnight in refrigerator. Delicious! I use this for shrimp cocktail and in salads.

CURRIED SHRIMP is my favorite. All you do is

Bec's Marinated Shrimp

3 lbs. shrimp	1 Tbl.
3 medium	Worchester-
onions	shire sauce
1 cup salad oil	salt and pepper
⅓ cup lemon	2 oz. crumbled
juice	bleu cheese

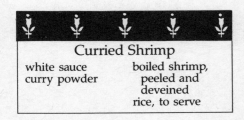

Curried Shrimp

white sauce	boiled shrimp,
curry powder	peeled and
	deveined
	rice, to serve

make a white sauce (see pg. 14), season it with curry powder, add lots of boiled shrimp, and serve on rice. Lots of people season crab and shrimp so highly that it loses its delicate flavor of fresh-caught seafood. I admit that much shipped seafood requires strong seasoning, but while on the coast use a light hand with condiments.

For **SEA ISLAND SHRIMP AND ONIONS**, place a layer of boiled shrimp, which have been peeled and deveined, in a deep pan or bowl. Cover thickly with rings of Spanish onion. Continue layers of shrimp and onion until all is used. Pour over this a generous amount of French dressing (see pg. 19) and a few capers. This should stand several hours until onion has absorbed dressing. Stir several times while it marinates. Eat with crisp crackers.

ST. SIMONS CHOWDER: This is a little trouble but do not let that discourage you, because on a cold night, when a Northeaster is blowing up, there's nothing that will take its place with a starving he-man. Be sure to ask at least 4 people to enjoy it with you. Make a peach pie for dessert and serve tons of crisp crackers, and you've got a treat.

Cut ½ lb. of streak o' lean fat into small cubes, and brown in skillet. Add 4 cups chopped onions and 1 chopped bell pepper, and stir until tender and fairly well browned. Now, add 2 cups water, 2 bouillon cubes (unless you have some stock), and 2 cups diced Irish potatoes. Cover and *simmer* about 10 minutes or until potatoes are tender. Add 1 qt. sweet milk, and a dash of salt and pepper. Next, add 1 lb. green shrimp, cleaned and cut into small pieces, to chowder. Then, when shrimp are pink and done (about 5 minutes), add ½ lb. or 2 cups cooked crab meat. Pour into soup tureen or individual deep bowls and start eating. The second and third helpings are better than the first! Serves 6 to 8. You may use cooked shrimp, and canned crab, or boiled lobster. If you have no seafood, pour in a can of creamed corn just before serving. Clams and scallops are also wonderful in this and I have even used

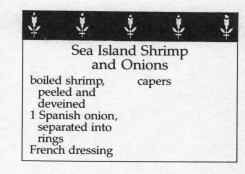

Sea Island Shrimp and Onions

boiled shrimp, peeled and deveined
1 Spanish onion, separated into rings
French dressing
capers

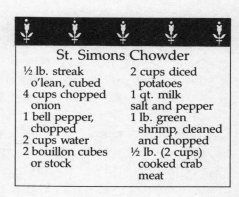

St. Simons Chowder

½ lb. streak o'lean, cubed
4 cups chopped onion
1 bell pepper, chopped
2 cups water
2 bouillon cubes or stock
2 cups diced potatoes
1 qt. milk
salt and pepper
1 lb. green shrimp, cleaned and chopped
½ lb. (2 cups) cooked crab meat

oysters and fish with success.

For **DARIEN SHRIMP**, into a heavy pot or skillet put 3 Tbl. prepared mustard, 1 sliced garlic button, 1 sliced onion, ½ cup Worchestershire sauce, 1 tsp. hot pepper, and the juice of 2 lemons. When this is hot, put in 3 lbs. green shrimp in the shells, sprinkle with salt, and as the shrimp turn pink, turn them often so the ones on the bottom won't overcook. Remove when all are pink (about 3 minutes) and drain in colander. Allow to cool. A real shrimp connoisseur prefers to eat them from the shell, prepared this way. Be sure to allow at least 1 lb. per person.

To prepare **FRIED GREEN SHRIMP**, remove shells, leaving tails on. Slit down back and remove black vein. The slit should be deep enough to lay open the shrimp. Wash, dry, and dip in flour. Fry in very hot oil, about 1-inch deep. They should turn pink immediately and should not cook longer than 5 minutes, so do not put over 8 in skillet at a time. These are best with hot grits, but since grits have become a shortage, you may have to substitute baked Irish potatoes. Have plenty of **TARTAR SAUCE** (mayonnaise to which has been added chopped onion, chopped bell pepper, capers, and lemon juice) or use a **COCKTAIL SAUCE** (chili sauce flavored with 1 Tbl. grated horseradish) for dipping.

HAM SLICE WITH FRUIT: When in the mood for ham, buy a ½-inch thick slice. Use only half of it if no company is coming. Trim, and toss on hot skillet until browned on one side, then turn. This takes only about 10 or 15 minutes. Remove from fire, add water to pan and make gravy. Brown in butter any 2 fruit halves (peaches or apricots, sliced pineapple or pears) and place them around ham. If there are not enough points for canned fruits, try broiled apple slices, broiled bananas, or sliced sweet potatoes. Add hot bread and coffee and you've a grand meal.

I am including **VEAL BIRDS** because they are excellent at the coast, having such a gamey flavor.

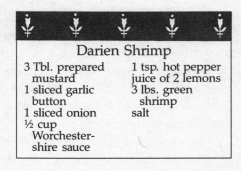

Darien Shrimp

3 Tbl. prepared mustard	1 tsp. hot pepper
1 sliced garlic button	juice of 2 lemons
1 sliced onion	3 lbs. green shrimp
½ cup Worchestershire sauce	salt

Fried Green Shrimp

green shrimp	hot oil
flour	tartar sauce or cocktail sauce, to serve

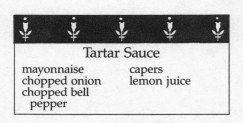

Tartar Sauce

mayonnaise	capers
chopped onion	lemon juice
chopped bell pepper	

Cocktail Sauce

chili sauce	1 Tbl. grated horseradish

Ham Slice with Fruit

1 ½-inch thick ham slice	2 types of fruit, halved or sliced
water	butter

When you see a fine-looking piece of rich, red, round steak, do buy a piece about ½-inch thick and let it be a "Veal Bird Night." Cut the steak in 4-inch wide slices about 5 or 6 inches in length. Put several anchovies over the top or spread with anchovy paste. Roll the steak up and stick toothpicks in it to hold it together. Cut a tomato in half (unpeeled) and pin one half to the top of each roll with toothpicks, always leaving enough of the pick showing so that you can pull it out easily when done. Put the rolled steaks in your baking dish. Pour over them 1 cup olive oil and drop in 2 bay leaves. Add salt, cover, and cook at 300° 1 hour. They look like red birds and taste like wild duck or marsh hen. I have never decided why they are called veal birds but you may serve them to the Colonel and the Colonel's lady with no hesitation. But never, never tell what they are; that's a family secret. Allow 1½ lb. of steak to each bird.

For a **FRUIT DESSERT**, slice fresh pineapple in half lengthwise. Remove core. Scoop out fruit. Cut into small slices or squares. Mix together with orange or grapefruit sections, diced apples, sliced bananas, cherries, grapes, berries, or a combination of any fresh fruits. Sprinkle with sugar. Season with sherry and lemon juice. Fill pineapple shells. May serve 1 small half to each person or pass large halves to 4.

While you are located where you can get plenty of fat, yard-raised chicken it is an excellent time to serve **FRIED CHICKEN**. Have a heavy skillet with cooking oil or lard 1-inch deep piping hot. Cut a 2-lb. chicken for frying. Wash and dry well. Salt, and roll in flour. Drop into hot fat, turning until all sides are brown. Cover, lower heat, and cook about 20 minutes until tender. Remove to drain on brown paper. Serve hot or cold. Serves 2-4.

To make **CHICKEN GRAVY**, pour off most of the fat, leaving browned flour in pan. Add 2 Tbl. flour, and salt and pepper. When flour is brown, add 2

Veal Birds (Steak)

round steak, ½-inch thick	1 cup olive oil
anchovies or anchovy paste	2 bay leaves
1 tomato	salt

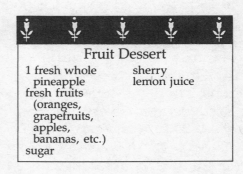

Fruit Dessert

1 fresh whole pineapple	sherry
fresh fruits (oranges, grapefruits, apples, bananas, etc.)	lemon juice
sugar	

Fried Chicken

cooking oil or lard	salt
1 2-lb. chicken	flour

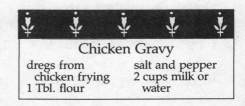

Chicken Gravy

dregs from chicken frying	salt and pepper
1 Tbl. flour	2 cups milk or water

cups milk or water and cook slowly until thickened. Serve with dry rice. Please have hot biscuits!

LEFTOVER FRIED CHICKEN CASSEROLE: Put your leftover fried chicken into a casserole dish and cover with sweet milk. Season with butter and salt and pepper. Bake in 350° oven until milk forms a good gravy (about 30 minutes).

My most popular recipe with chicken is **BANANA FRITTERS** with orange sauce. Practice these because they are delicious as you know! Mash 4 bananas slightly. Stir with 3 Tbl. flour, 3 eggs, 1 Tbl. sugar, salt, and 2 tsp. baking powder. Add just enough milk to make a batter. It should be thick enough to drop by tablespoonfuls into hot grease and hold together. If you should get it too thin, add a little more flour. Prepare hot oil about 3 inches deep in a small pan. Drop tablespoonfuls of batter into pan. Cook quickly until brown on one side and roll over. You need rather high heat, because every time you drop another fritter in, it cools down a little. Watch closely to see that they do not burn. Only cook 2 or 3 at a time. Drain on paper when done. Keep warm in a very low oven if necessary. Makes about 20 fritters. Serve with Tart Orange Sauce.

TART ORANGE SAUCE: Mix 1 tsp. lemon juice, 3 Tbl. butter, 1 cup orange juice (or juice and grated rind of 2 oranges), ¾ cup sugar, and 3 tsp. cornstarch. Boil mixture while stirring constantly until thick and transparent (about 5 minutes). Makes 2 cups.

WAFFLES: Treasure this recipe because it is the only copy in existence. It was the result of a day's experimenting. I never had tasted a waffle I thought tasted like a waffle ought to taste, so I determined to find out why. I wasted plenty of material working it out, but considering the twenty-five years of waffles we've enjoyed, I think the end justified the means.

Since I always started with a quart of milk, I usually had batter left over, and it has proved a godsend as we've learned to use it in so many ways. For

Leftover Fried Chicken Casserole

fried chicken	butter
milk	salt and pepper

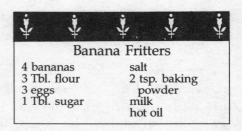

Banana Fritters

4 bananas	salt
3 Tbl. flour	2 tsp. baking
3 eggs	powder
1 Tbl. sugar	milk
	hot oil

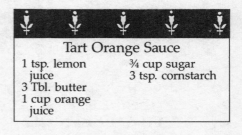

Tart Orange Sauce

1 tsp. lemon juice	¾ cup sugar
3 Tbl. butter	3 tsp. cornstarch
1 cup orange juice	

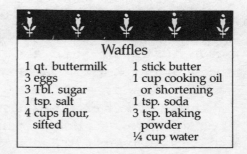

Waffles

1 qt. buttermilk	1 stick butter
3 eggs	1 cup cooking oil
3 Tbl. sugar	or shortening
1 tsp. salt	1 tsp. soda
4 cups flour, sifted	3 tsp. baking
	powder
	¼ cup water

instance, you can add more flour to make a stiffer dough, then add a pinch more baking powder and you have wonderful muffins. Add blueberries, raisins, cherries, nuts, grated cheese, etc., to this, and you have variety in muffins. Or dip slices of cucumber, squash, okra, or tomato in a bit of the leftover batter and fry, and out comes a tasty vegetable fritter. (Always add 1 tsp. of baking powder to leftover batter, as the original has lost its effectiveness.) And don't forget the sauces for the fritters. The leftover batter also makes crepes suzettes (see pg. 80) or battercakes (see pg. 81-82) for lunch or breakfast.

So, make the whole recipe and you are prepared for any expediency. The batter improves as it stays in the ice box. We make ours up in the morning if we are having them for supper, the night before if for breakfast, because it must stay in the ice box until the shortening is very cold. Do not put in baking powder until ready to cook. After your waffle iron has been greased once, do not grease again, as the fat in the batter is sufficient. Start heating iron about 15 minutes before needed, so it can be smoking hot. After you have finished cooking waffles, let iron cool and wipe off with damp cloth. Never let water get in coils.

Now for the recipe: Put 1 qt. buttermilk in large mixing bowl. Into this, break 3 whole eggs and beat together. Add 3 Tbl. sugar and 1 tsp. salt. Mix. Have 4 cups sifted flour ready and stir into this mixture until all is in. Now beat — beat hard and furiously for 5 or 6 minutes. Melt in a skillet 1 stick butter and 1 cup cooking oil or shortening. Add to waffle mixture, beat some more, and put in ice box for at least 4 hours.

When ready to cook, add 1 tsp. soda and 3 tsp. baking powder dissolved in ¼ cup water. As batter puffs up, start cooking in hot iron, putting in only 2 Tbl. at a time. If this amount does not make a complete waffle, add more next time. One big kitchen

spoonful is usually about right; if too much is used, batter runs out on the sides. Do not open the iron until the steam stops pouring out. By this time they should be golden brown, crisp, and delicious. If you are not sure when they are done, open the iron just enough to peek. You'll soon learn, and they are much better if not disturbed. Sweet milk may be used, omitting soda, but they are not as crisp this way. (Remember to add another teaspoon of baking powder to leftover batter.) Makes 8 or 10.

CREPES SUZETTES (Mother's Way): Your Uncle Joe delights in making crepes suzettes at the table in his chafing dish on Sunday nights. He really does it with a flair too, and your mouth is watering long before you get one. He refuses to make them for more than 4 people, and he's right about that, too. But I never have as few as 4 around my table, so I had to figure out a way to make them wholesale. They melt in your mouth, and most of the men in our family can eat 6 after a big meal.

So, the proof of the pudding: For this, refer to my waffle recipe above. Divide waffle batter in half. Add enough cream to one half to thin it just a little. Add 2 more Tbl. sugar and 1 more tsp. baking powder than is used for waffles. Have a griddle hot, but not *too* hot. Grease with butter or cooking oil and drop batter in by teaspoonfuls. Do not crowd. When cakes begin to bubble, turn with cake turner and sprinkle top sides with powdered sugar. Cakes should be very thin. When cakes are brown on bottom, remove to hot plate, roll into tight little rolls, and secure with toothpicks. Continue to cook cakes as fast as you can. When you have enough stacked, one on the other, sprinkle with powdered sugar and cover with napkin. Put where they will keep warm until served. Make lots of rum sauce (see pg. 14) and have it piping hot. When ready to serve, place 3 or 4 rolls (after removing toothpicks) on a hot dessert plate. Pour sauce over them and serve at once. Serves 8-10.

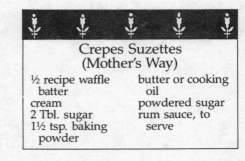

Crepes Suzettes (Mother's Way)	
½ recipe waffle batter	butter or cooking oil
cream	powdered sugar
2 Tbl. sugar	rum sauce, to serve
1½ tsp. baking powder	

HOT CAKES MODERN: Put 1 cup prepared Bisquick in a mixing bowl, with 2 Tbl. corn meal, a pinch of salt, and 1 Tbl. sugar, and mix well. These ingredients may be sifted together. Break 1 egg, add to ½ cup milk, and beat until mixed. Pour this into the dry ingredients and mix, adding enough additional milk to make a batter the consistency of thick cream. Now dash in 2 Tbl. cooking oil or melted butter and when well mixed, add 2 tsp. baking powder, stirring just enough to combine well.

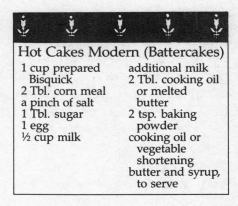

Hot Cakes Modern (Battercakes)

1 cup prepared Bisquick	additional milk
2 Tbl. corn meal	2 Tbl. cooking oil or melted butter
a pinch of salt	
1 Tbl. sugar	2 tsp. baking powder
1 egg	cooking oil or vegetable shortening
½ cup milk	butter and syrup, to serve

Since you probably haven't got a griddle, use your heaviest frying pan. Have it hot all over, but not as hot as for a steak. Add enough cooking oil or vegetable shortening to barely cover bottom of pan. Drop batter into pan in spoonfuls, the size depending upon your own taste (we prefer them about 4 inches across). They should immediately begin to bubble up all over. If they do not, then the pan is not hot enough. If they smoke, the pan is too hot. By the time the whole surface is bubbled up they should be brown on the bottom, so turn them quickly, and as soon as they are brown on that side, remove to small plate and stack in piles of 3. Serve them fast — while hot. Do not ever turn a battercake more than once. These are simply wonderful with butter and syrup. Serves 2.

Back in the old days in Athens when eggs were ten cents a dozen, Mama used to make a fruit pudding for Papa's special guests that in my estimation has never been equaled. She made a sponge cake with fourteen eggs and a custard with as many more, and skimmed cream ½-inch thick off the milk and whipped it, and used cups of old wine papa had brought all the way from France and half a dozen kinds of fruit and at least two kinds of nuts. Someday maybe we can get enough together for her to make us another one. She had to pack hers in tubs of ice and salt as she had no freezing unit. I've

invented an imitation which is far from the original, but still better than most desserts and easy to make.

HEAVENLY DESSERT: Buy a small pound cake at the grocer's. Have several kinds of fruit, whether canned or fresh: peaches, grapes, pears, pineapple, bananas, raspberries, strawberries, cherries — any 3 will do. Assemble about 2 cups total. Mash fruits slightly and keep separate. Make 2 cups boiled custard (see pg. 72) and when cool, flavor with sherry. Have some nuts (½ cup or more) chopped up: pecans, walnuts, almonds (anything but peanuts).

Take your largest freezing pan or loaf bread pan and pour a little custard in bottom. Put thin slices of pound cake over this, more custard over the cake, then put a layer of one of the fruits and nuts over this, more custard, then another layer of cake, until all fruits, nuts, custard, and cake have been used. Freeze. Serve on platter with whipped cream. Slice it like a layer cake and sit back and listen to everybody rave! Serves 8.

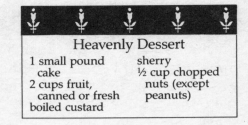

Heavenly Dessert

1 small pound cake	sherry
2 cups fruit, canned or fresh	½ cup chopped nuts (except peanuts)
boiled custard	

Dick will probably think I've lost my mind, sending this last dessert, but once he gets a taste of it he'll not begrudge the ingredients. Even thinking of it has made me forget for awhile the war and its multitude of worries. Eating it could do no less! So, darling, be generous with foods now while Dick is on this side to enjoy them. We can skimp and save when he's across the waters eating rations, but with happy memories at the thought of your good cooking.

I do hope we can catch the train down for a weekend soon. Will take you and Dick to the Frederica Yacht Club for a steak. I don't know any other place else where we can get one. The view over the river there is so beautiful. I really can't wait!!

Much love to you and Dick,
Mother

Atlanta, Georgia
September 24, 1942

Selma darling:

I was distressed to hear that all my good shrimp recipes will have to wait. I should have realized that the shrimp boats cannot go out while this submarine war is on. How war changes everything — even the life of a shrimp.

However, since crab is plentiful and Dick likes all your crab dishes, you won't miss the shrimp recipes and you'll probably save money and ration points. It is so difficult to find recipes which can be made with so many things to consider — what with ration points, the scarcity of certain foods, and the complete disappearance of others. But if you are smart you will find ways to substitute and learn how to save points on one meal in order to have point foods in another. Even Bella has accepted prepared Bisquick, but unless I watch her she will slip in a little more lard. Everytime I go to the store I find new, prepared foods which save time and points. I have a time getting the Mistress of the Kitchen to use them, though!

Since shrimp is out of the picture for the present, why not give Dick a crab beach supper for his birthday? The blackout eliminates the best part — having a driftwood fire — but it can be managed anyway, provided your guests come early and are well finished at sunset. You boil and prepare your crabs at home, so the boys can help you get them on the beach with no trouble. Chill your beer in a dish pan or tub and carry it to the beach that way. It will easily fit in the trunk of the car. Crisp your crackers and have plenty of them, along with a bowl of pickles and sticks of carrots and celery in a bowl with ice over them. Take one or two bridge tables, a cloth for each, and a package of paper napkins. Don't forget

the bottle opener. Count on 8 to 12 crabs per person, so get one of your friends to help you catch them. Have everything ready to put into the car when Dick comes home and the guests assemble at your house.

BEACH PARTY CRAB: Boil and clean crabs (see pg. 67) at home. Take out to the beach and place on large platter. Surround with claws. Put a big pan on the table for shells and membranes and let everyone pick out his own meat. Serve with melted butter and crackers.

Though not a requisite, a huge bowl of **SEA SHELL SALAD** would not be amiss. Cook 1 cup shell macaroni in boiling salted water. Drain carefully and cool. When cool mix with the following, (all chopped): ½ cup green olives, ½ cup ripe olives, 2 hard-boiled eggs, ½ cup green pepper, 1 slice pimento, ½ cup celery, and ¼ cup onion. Blend together with mayonnaise, and salt to taste. Chill 4 hours before serving. Serves 6 to 8.

Try this for Sunday dinner — **FILLET OF FLOUNDER IN WHITE WINE**: Put 2 fillets in a glass baking dish. Add dots of butter, sliced mushrooms, a few small cooked onions, salt and pepper, a bay leaf, and a sprig of thyme. Pour about 4 oz. of dry white wine in dish, and bake in a 350° oven until tender (about 20 minutes), basting occasionally. Brown a moment under flame and serve with lemon. Serves 2.

Do not have the next recipe with flounder but try it the next time you have guests. **WEINSCHAUM PUDDING**: Cook in double boiler (being careful not to let the top boiler touch boiling water in lower part) 2 cups white wine, ½ cup water, 4 unbeaten eggs, and ½ cup sugar. Beat vigorously and constantly until thickened. Serve hot or cold. Serves 4 to 6.

I feel that it is almost a waste of time to give you the cake recipes requested, because those cakes simply have to have loads of butter, eggs, and sugar and I

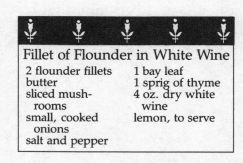

Sea Shell Salad

1 cup shell macaroni	1 slice pimento, chopped
salt	½ cup chopped celery
½ cup green olives, chopped	¼ cup chopped onion
½ cup ripe olives, chopped	mayonnaise
2 hard-boiled eggs, chopped	salt
¼ cup chopped green pepper	

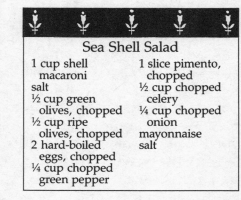

Fillet of Flounder in White Wine

2 flounder fillets	1 bay leaf
butter	1 sprig of thyme
sliced mushrooms	4 oz. dry white wine
small, cooked onions	lemon, to serve
salt and pepper	

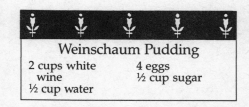

Weinschaum Pudding

2 cups white wine	4 eggs
½ cup water	½ cup sugar

might as well tell you to use frankincence and myrrh!

Of course, there are cakes that you can make, even in these times, and I shall give you some recipes for these, but please remember these are merely substitutes for honest cakes. When the war is over, I'll teach you to make the kind you've always loved, the kind I learned to bake down at Oxford in Aunt Emmie's kitchen.

My, what a cake baking *that* was every Friday afternoon! Old Uncle Richard carried all the ingredients out to the back porch where the tremendous scales were kept. He had a huge earthenware mixing bowl. It must have had a five gallon capacity. He'd weigh out three pounds of sweet, fresh-churned butter and weigh five pounds of sugar from the barrel. These he would cream until all sugar was melted. Three dozen eggs fresh from the nest were broken into this, then flour (five pounds in all) was sifted in alternately with a quart of sweet milk right from the cow. Baking powder and vanilla were added after the batter was as smooth as velvet.

Fat pine sticks, dripping with rosin, were piled into the fire box of the stove until the oven was so hot, his hand could only be held inside long enough to count six. By this time, layer cake pans had been filled and four were placed on the lower rack; as these rose they were moved to the top rack and four more placed on the bottom.

We children stood around fascinated, trying not to get in the way, drinking in the fragrance of the baking cakes, our eyes glued on the big bowl and on Uncle Richard as he dashed around in his starched apron and cap that always looked so white compared to his smiling black face.

At this point, Aunt Emmie arrived (the aroma of the first cakes had permeated the living room). She tied a snow white apron around her waist, gave us children a big, reassuring smile, and went to work. She completely covered the big kitchen table with

smooth linen towels. Over part of these she spread the leaves from a huge spray of lemon verbena; on the next part she lay rose geranium leaves; and on the last part mint leaves were placed close together. Over all these leaves she generously sprinkled sugar.

Uncle Richard took out the first four layers and turned them out over the lemon verbena leaves and we crowded close to breathe in the heavenly fragrance that seeped up through those cakes. No perfumes of Araby could compare with the perfumes that floated up to us as the hot cake absorbed the oils of the pungent leaves. While Uncle Richard gently placed more cakes in the stove as he removed the first, Aunt Emmie sliced a hot brown layer into wedges, the number of slices depending upon the number of eagerly awaiting children. Oh, how wonderful it was!

When sixteen layers had been cooked, Uncle Richard got out the little spice mill and dumped into it whole cloves, cinnamon sticks, nutmeg, and all kinds of other spices and ground them into a powder. These he dashed lavishly into the batter remaining in the big bowl, mixed it in thoroughly and spooned the batter into layer pans, leaving a generous portion in the bottom and all around the sides of the bowl for us. For some reason, Joe always got the spoon to lick, and it was tremendous and half full of batter! How I envied him, because the rest of us had to work fast to get our share from the bowl.

It is amazing to me in this enlightened day that we were not all sick every Friday night while at Aunt Emmie's, because we certainly gorged ourselves on raw cake batter and icings of every description. But we survived without pain and I still like to "lick the bowl" — it's never hurt you either!

While the last cakes were cooking, Aunt Emmie started the icings and fillings — chocolate, caramel, lemon cheese, coconut, and white mountain, and as the last spice layer came out of the stove, the lemon

cheese was being iced.

At long last, five four-layer cakes were finished, iced to the Queen's taste, and set on tall glass cake stands with glass covers, and all placed on the high-boy in the darkened dining room to await the arrival of a guest.

I wish I could give you some idea of how those cakes tasted, some picture of the way they looked when sliced on a silver platter. The spice cake was my favorite — the filling of raisins, nuts, citron, coconut and currants, held together with a butter frosting, was like nothing else I've ever tasted.

I think the fact that you long to make good cakes, because there are always so many hungry Marines dropping in, is sure proof that you are indeed sharing the fruits of your labors. And I'm proud and happy over this, as it displays not only a generosity of heart, but that you are a gracious hostess. And that is an asset that will be of untold value to your husband as he makes his way in a world of competition when the war is won.

The following **RULES FOR CAKE BAKING** may simplify things for you. Set on your table all the ingredients named in the recipe and all the utensils used. Use the best materials, eggs, etc. Measure accurately, using standard measuring spoons and cups. Mix carefully. Make sure oven temperature is right, and to test cake when done stick a clean straw in thickest part and if it comes out clean the cake is done. Sift granulated sugar if lumpy, and sift flour on waxed paper to eliminate extra washing of bowls. Let shortening stand at room temperature awhile before using, so that it will cream more easily and quickly, but never melt. Place filled pans as near the center of the oven as possible, as heat is more even there.

Little Alice's gang still has a sweet tooth, in spite of sugar shortages, so Bella and I keep one or two of

these in the box. We've christened them **WAR CAKES**. They really are good and take only about five minutes to make, so you might try them.

Buy a pound cake at the grocer's, and slice it into 6 thin slices, longways. Make an icing by adding 3 egg yolks and the juice and grated rind of 4 lemons to 1 can of sweetened condensed milk. Stir and spread on layers using only 3 layers to a cake so the slices will be a nice size. Set in ice box about an hour before serving. This gives you 2 cakes.

For chocolate layer cake use the same recipe as for War Cake. Spread German Chocolate Fudge frosting between layers and on top. Decorate with pecans if desired.

GERMAN CHOCOLATE FUDGE FROSTING: Whip 3 egg whites slightly. Melt 1 stick butter or margarine and 4 packages (or 1 lb.) semi-sweet German chocolate over hot water in double boiler. Add to eggs. Sift in 1½ boxes XXXX sugar. Add a pinch of salt and 1 tsp. vanilla extract. Beat until smooth. Thin if necessary with milk or cream.

PINEAPPLE UPSIDE-DOWN CAKE: Preheat oven to 350°. Sift 1¼ cups flour, measure once and add 1¼ tsp. baking powder, ¼ tsp. salt, and ¾ cup granulated sugar, and sift together 3 times. Add 4 Tbl. creamed butter. Add 1 beaten egg, ½ cup milk, and 1 tsp. vanilla extract to flour mixture, stirring well. Beat vigorously for 1 minute. Now melt 4 Tbl. butter in 9-inch iron skillet over low flame. Add ½ cup brown sugar and stir until mixed. On top, arrange 4 pineapple slices and sprinkle 1 cup broken pecan meats over these. Turn batter out onto contents of skillet. Bake 50 minutes. Turn upside down on dish with pineapple on top and serve with whipped cream, if desired. Or to be accurate, if you can *get* it! Serves 8.

ANGEL FOOD CAKE: Measurements for this are, 1¼ cups sifted cake flour, 1¼ cups granulated sugar, 1 cup egg whites, ¼ tsp. salt, 1 tsp. cream of tartar, ¾ tsp. vanilla extract, and ¼ tsp. almond

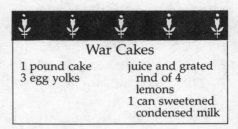

War Cakes

1 pound cake	juice and grated rind of 4 lemons
3 egg yolks	1 can sweetened condensed milk

German Chocolate Fudge Frosting

3 egg whites, beaten slightly	pinch of salt
1 stick butter or margarine	1 tsp. vanilla extract
4 packages (or 1 lb.) semi-sweet German chocolate	milk or cream, if necessary
1½ boxes XXXX sugar	

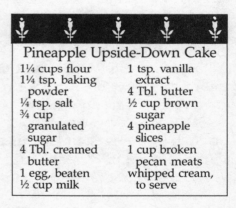

Pineapple Upside-Down Cake

1¼ cups flour	1 tsp. vanilla extract
1¼ tsp. baking powder	4 Tbl. butter
¼ tsp. salt	½ cup brown sugar
¾ cup granulated sugar	4 pineapple slices
4 Tbl. creamed butter	1 cup broken pecan meats
1 egg, beaten	whipped cream, to serve
½ cup milk	

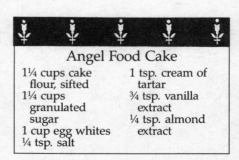

Angel Food Cake

1¼ cups cake flour, sifted	1 tsp. cream of tartar
1¼ cups granulated sugar	¾ tsp. vanilla extract
1 cup egg whites	¼ tsp. almond extract
¼ tsp. salt	

extract. Sift 1 cup flour once. Measure. Add ¼ cup sugar and sift together four times. Beat egg whites and salt together with wire egg beater. When foamy, add cream of tartar and continue beating until eggs are stiff enough to hold up in peaks but not dry. Add remaining 1 cup sugar, 2 Tbl. at a time, beating with wire egg beater after each addition until sugar is *just* blended. Fold in flavoring. Then sift ¼ cup flour over mixture and fold in lightly. Turn into ungreased Angel Food pan and cut gently through batter with knife to remove air bubbles. Place in cold oven and bake at 325°, 45 to 50 minutes. Remove from oven and invert pan until cake is cold — about 1 hour. Serves 8.

CHOCOLATE MINT ROLL: Preheat oven to 400°. Sift 6 Tbl. cake flour once. Measure. Sift with ½ tsp. baking powder and ¼ tsp. salt. Sift together 3 times. Fold ¾ cup sugar into 4 stiffly beaten egg whites. Then fold in 4 egg yolks which have been beaten until stiff and lemon-colored. Add 1 tsp. vanilla extract and fold in flour mixture gradually. Then beat in 2 squares unsweetened chocolate (melted) and turn into greased 11-inch-by-17-inch jelly roll pan or cookie sheet with sides. Bake in 400° oven for about 15 minutes. Quickly cut off crisp edges of cake and turn out on cloth covered with powdered sugar. Spread half of mint frosting over cake and roll as for jelly roll. Wrap in cloth and cool about 5 minutes. Cover roll with remaining frosting. Serves 8 to 10.

MINT FROSTING: Break 3 egg whites in a bowl and beat slightly. Add 4 Tbl. melted butter. Beat into this 1 box XXXX sugar. Stir and put in ½ tsp. peppermint flavoring.

I believe this covers the territory for the moment.

With much love,
Mother

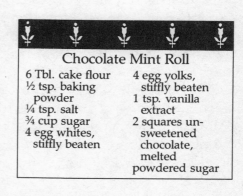

Chocolate Mint Roll

6 Tbl. cake flour	4 egg yolks, stiffly beaten
½ tsp. baking powder	1 tsp. vanilla extract
¼ tsp. salt	2 squares unsweetened chocolate, melted
¾ cup sugar	powdered sugar
4 egg whites, stiffly beaten	

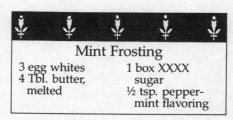

Mint Frosting

3 egg whites	1 box XXXX sugar
4 Tbl. butter, melted	½ tsp. peppermint flavoring

Atlanta, Georgia
October 15, 1942

Selma darling:

We were amazed at the sudden move to Cherry Point. How on earth could you get away in twenty-four hours?

Of course you're disappointed not to get a house on Officer's Row, in the Flats, or even in the project outside the gates. What a crowd there must be. However, it is encouraging to know there is hope of a vacancy soon, and that you found a place only forty miles away at New Bern.

Your desperate effort to sound cheerful in spite of your drooping spirits fairly wrung my heart. Daddy reassures me by predicting that when you receive this letter he knows you will be back to normal, and more than likely will have become acquainted with every citizen in New Bern. I hope he's right.

No matter how hopeless it looks now, I know your clever hands will have the place looking lovely in a few days. How I wish I could be there to help you. It is a good thing Dick is handy around the house, since you move so often. Get him to fix you up a painted orange crate and find a place in your cubbyhole kitchen for it. It will be perfect to hold your precious box of accessories and wonderfully convenient.

Don't let a tiny kitchen and no dining room discourage you or force Dick into short rations. Try to have casserole dishes and things that will cook in a hurry, like steaks. Plan your meals so that you won't fall all over yourself and the dishes trying to get a million things done at the last minute. Fix most of your supper in the mornings. Have your vegetables cleaned, cut, and ready to cook. Make your desserts and salads. Have your casserole ready to run into the oven. Do all the dirty work in the mornings, so your kitchen won't be cluttered at dinner time.

The gaily flowered oil cloth sounds like a nice

antidote to the drab walls and furnishings. The wood stove in the living room probably offends your aesthetic eye, but I'll bet it feels pretty comfortable these chilly nights. If you had the pleasant memories of wood burning stoves that I have from the old house on the campus in Athens, you'd hug the one in your bedroom as if it were an old, old friend! I guess you're right about the "drupy" wallpaper. The best thing to do is to walk out and leave it as often as possible. Still it is home, Sugar, and Dick comes back to it each evening, so don't let it get you down. I know you don't.

New Bern is filled with antiques and fine old homes. Get out and hunt some old glass or find some mustache cups for my collection. I'll reimburse you for any you send. And why not do some watercolors of the waterfront? There should be some picturesque scenes to inspire you.

The enclosed recipes will make grand dinners for Dick and keep your mind off the wallpaper, and the sagging iron bed. So first — find a shad.

BAKED SHAD: Buy a nice shad and stuff tight with a dressing of mashed potatoes or dry bread crumbs with butter, chopped parsley, and salt and pepper. Fasten sides together with toothpicks or needle and coarse thread. Sprinkle with salt and pepper, dredge in flour, and cover with slice of bacon. Wrap in piece of cheese cloth, put in roasting pan and cover bottom with about 1 inch of water. Bake 15 minutes per lb. in 400° oven. Add more water if necessary. Serve with lemon and butter sauce or Fish Hollandaise (see pg. 15).

For **FRIED TOMATOES**, slice unpeeled, firm tomatoes into thick slices. Coat thickly with white corn meal and fry in bacon drippings. If your fat is too deep, they will not brown and will become soggy and break. If not deep enough, the meal will burn, so experiment a little. I use just enough to cover the

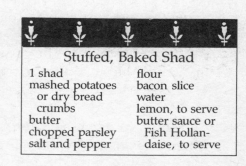

Stuffed, Baked Shad

1 shad	flour
mashed potatoes or dry bread crumbs	bacon slice
	water
	lemon, to serve
butter	butter sauce or
chopped parsley	Fish Hollandaise, to serve
salt and pepper	

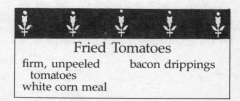

Fried Tomatoes

firm, unpeeled tomatoes	bacon drippings
white corn meal	

bottom of the pan and add more as needed. They should brown on one side in 2 minutes, then turn them over. Better cook plenty the first time — unless I miss my guess they'll prove popular. They should be crisp on the outside and tender in the center. As you remember, we serve these at breakfast, lunch, or dinner as they pep up any meal. Even green tomatoes may be used this way. These are crisper if you coat with meal and put in refrigerator to sit awhile. Don't add salt and pepper until after cooking.

I fix **FRIED EGGPLANT** the same way — slice it in ½-inch slices (leave peel on) and soak a few minutes in salt water to remove bitter acid. Dry. Dip in meal and fry the same as tomatoes, or, if you prefer, cut it as you do French fried potatoes (peel). Of course, you know Daddy's favorite dish is eggplant stuffed with oysters, but since you are not especially enthusiastic about oysters, I won't bother to give you the recipe. Write me if you'd like it.

To prepare **BEEF STEW WITH DUMPLINGS**, cut 1 lb. chuck into 1-inch cubes, dredge in flour, and sauté in fat or drippings from the suet. Sauté a small, sliced onion and peel and cube a small carrot and ¼ turnip. Put all together in skillet. Add 1 cup water, stock, or strained canned tomatoes, salt and pepper, and 1 small, sliced potato. Cover and cook over low heat until tender (about 1 hour).

Dumplings: Mix 1 cup flour, 1 tsp. salt, 1 tsp. baking powder, and 2 Tbl. water. Drop by spoonfuls into stew when almost done. Cover and steam 10 minutes. Do not remove cover during cooking. Add ½ cup water to stew, if necessary, to make gravy for the dumplings. Serve with dumplings arranged around the edges of a platter and stew in the middle. Serves 2.

CHICKEN MOLD: Make 2 cups thick well-seasoned white sauce. Cut up meat from a boiled hen or fryer until you have 2 cups. Break 2 eggs into white sauce and mix well. Add chicken, 1 can mushrooms,

Fried Eggplant

eggplant	meal
salted water	bacon drippings

Beef Stew with Dumplings

1 lb. chuck, cubed	salt and pepper
flour	1 small potato, sliced
fat or suet drippings	1 cup flour
1 small onion, sliced	1 tsp. salt
1 small carrot	1 tsp. baking powder
¼ turnip	2 Tbl. water
1 cup water, stock, or strained tomatoes	½ cup water, if necessary

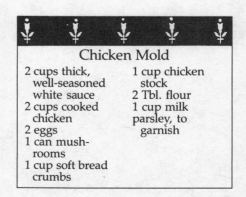

Chicken Mold

2 cups thick, well-seasoned white sauce	1 cup chicken stock
2 cups cooked chicken	2 Tbl. flour
2 eggs	1 cup milk
1 can mushrooms	parsley, to garnish
1 cup soft bread crumbs	

and 1 cup of soft bread crumbs. Put in buttered loaf pan and bake at 350° about 40 minutes until firm. Turn out onto platter and serve with a sauce made of 1 cup chicken stock, 2 Tbl. flour, and 1 cup milk. Cook until it thickens. Add more mushrooms and pour over loaf. Garnish with parsley. Sliced almonds add a zip to this but are not essential. Serves 6 to 8.

CHICKEN SALAD: Cut chicken into small pieces. Do not use fat. Chill. Add mayonnaise, chopped celery, and chopped nuts. Mix well.

To serve **BROILED SHAD ROE**, season well, dip in melted butter, and place under broiler (not too close to flame). Brown slowly and serve with bacon and lemon. Or sauté in butter in skillet.

For a wonderful supper-in-a-hurry try **EGGS BENEDICT**. Broil thin slices of ham (or use a can of devilled ham). Poach 2 eggs per person. Arrange ham on slices of toast, or, better still, Holland rusks or toasted English muffins. Top with egg and cover with Hollandaise sauce (see pg. 15). Toss together a crisp salad and there's a meal.

Save up your ration points and treat Dick to a **PLANKED STEAK**. I'll send the planks right away. They are new so you'll have to season them. Just rub metal surfaces with oil, then with salt, and heat slowly in the oven. Do this for 3 days.

When your planks are ready, buy 2 club steaks about 1-inch or 1½-inches thick and remove the bone. Heat your metal planks and when they are piping hot, slap on the steaks and put right under the flame of the broiler. While the flame cooks one side, the plank will cook the other. Broil 15 minutes for medium rare. Salt and pepper. Serve steaks on metal planks set in wooden holders.

Serve your steaks with French fried onions (see below), and French fried potatoes (see pg. 6), and garnish with lettuce and tomato wedges. There you really have a man's favorite dinner! After this Dick won't complain about anything you give him for a week.

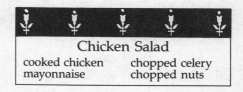

Chicken Salad

cooked chicken	chopped celery
mayonnaise	chopped nuts

Broiled Shad Roe

shad roe	bacon, to serve
seasonings	lemon, to serve
melted butter	

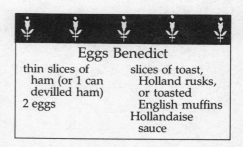

Eggs Benedict

thin slices of ham (or 1 can devilled ham)	slices of toast, Holland rusks, or toasted English muffins
2 eggs	Hollandaise sauce

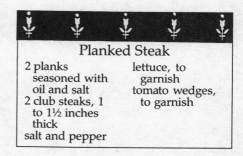

Planked Steak

2 planks seasoned with oil and salt	lettuce, to garnish
2 club steaks, 1 to 1½ inches thick	tomato wedges, to garnish
salt and pepper	

For a **TOMATO ENTREE**, spread Holland rusks with anchovy paste, cover with a large slice of tomato, top with Russian dressing, and sprinkle with grated hard-boiled egg topped by an olive. Run into hot oven to heat. Serve at once.

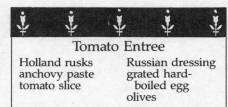

Tomato Entree	
Holland rusks	Russian dressing
anchovy paste	grated hard-
tomato slice	boiled egg
	olives

FRENCH FRIED ONIONS: Peel and slice 2 or 3 medium Spanish onions. Beat 1 egg into 1 cup milk. Dip slices in egg-milk and then in flour. Have frying pan or boiler half full of hot cooking oil or fat. Drop in a few onions at a time. Cook until golden brown. Drain on brown paper. Salt. To test fat, drop into it a small piece of white bread, if it browns quickly, fat is hot enough.

French Fried Onions	
2 or 3 medium	flour
Spanish onions	cooking oil or fat
1 egg	salt
1 cup milk	

Even if you are not a squash enthusiast, my **DELECTABLE BAKED SQUASH** recipe will convert you. Cut in half lengthwise 1 small or medium squash. Scoop out most of the seeds with spoon and boil squash for 10 minutes. Salt and pepper, and fill scooped-out centers with chopped onions, bread crumbs, dots of butter, and grated American cheese. Place ½ slice of bacon on top of each, and bake in 350° oven about 20 minutes, or until bacon is done. Add a little water to pan if necessary, to keep from burning.

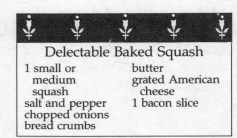

Delectable Baked Squash	
1 small or	butter
medium	grated American
squash	cheese
salt and pepper	1 bacon slice
chopped onions	
bread crumbs	

BELL PEPPER AND PIMENTO SALAD: Select a round, pretty pepper. Mix 1 3-oz. cream cheese with 1 tsp. plain gelatin dissolved in 1 Tbl. hot water. Chop 1 pimento fine. Cut off stem end of pepper and chop fine. Mix chopped pepper and pimento with cheese, and stuff hollowed-out pepper firmly with mixture. Chill in refrigerator. Slice on lettuce leaves. Serve about 3 slices per person. This is different and delicious! Serves 2.

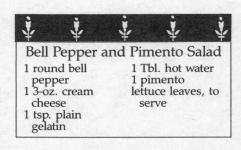

Bell Pepper and Pimento Salad	
1 round bell	1 Tbl. hot water
pepper	1 pimento
1 3-oz. cream	lettuce leaves, to
cheese	serve
1 tsp. plain	
gelatin	

To make **AUNT ALICE'S SPOON BREAD**, sift 1½ cups corn meal with 2 tsp. salt and 1 Tbl. sugar. Add 1 stick butter or margarine and pour on 1¼ cups boiling water. Stir to melt. Cool. Mix 1½ cups milk and 3 beaten eggs. Add to corn meal mixture. Then add 2 tsp. baking powder and mix well. Pour into a 2-qt. casserole and bake at 325° about 1 hour or until set

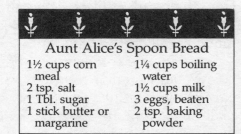

Aunt Alice's Spoon Bread	
1½ cups corn	1¼ cups boiling
meal	water
2 tsp. salt	1½ cups milk
1 Tbl. sugar	3 eggs, beaten
1 stick butter or	2 tsp. baking
margarine	powder

and brown on top. Serves 6 to 8.

BOILED DRY RICE: Put 2 cups water in top of double boiler and salt to taste. Add 1 cup rice and 1 Tbl. butter. Cover and place over hot water to cook. Rice is done when all the water has been cooked out. It will require about 45 minutes, but your rice will be dry and tender — just the way he likes it. Serves 4.

QUICK COFFEE DESSERT: Soak 2 envelopes plain gelatine in ½ cup cold water. Add 2 cups strong, hot coffee and sweeten to taste. Stir until gelatin is thoroughly dissolved. Add 1 cup thick cream and a little vanilla extract and pour into individual molds. (Makes about 6 small molds). Chill. To serve, unmold and cover with whipped cream.

For **PRUNE SOUFFLÉ**, use 2 egg whites, ⅓ cup corn syrup, 1 Tbl. sugar, ¼ tsp. salt, ⅛ tsp. cinnamon, 6 or 8 cooked or canned prunes (well-drained, cut, and mashed), and ½ cup chopped pecans. Combine unbeaten egg whites, syrup, sugar, salt, and cinnamon in bowl. Beat with rotary beater until mixture stands in peaks. Fold in prunes and nut meats. Turn into top of greased double boiler and cook over hot water 40 minutes without lifting top. Soufflé should double in bulk. Serve hot or cold with chilled custard sauce made using the 2 egg yolks. Custard sauce is ½ recipe boiled custard (see pg. 72). Serves 6.

Now, I know you'll faint when I suggest that you try making **BAKED ALASKA**. You'll have visions of those huge, gorgeous confections we used to have at the Driving Club. But I've made it many times and even now that I cannot make the cake for lack of materials, I still make it with short-cuts and improvisions on the original recipe. It is delicious and easy.

Buy a rectangular pound cake (the 1-lb. size) at the store. The cake must first be hollowed out to form a boxlike structure in which to hold layers of fruit and ice cream. To do this, take a sharp knife and cut a ½-inch layer from the top of the cake. This will be used as the lid of the box later, so set it aside. Now, carefully cut down all four sides of the cake, to form

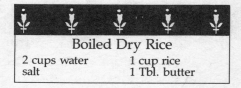

Boiled Dry Rice

2 cups water	1 cup rice
salt	1 Tbl. butter

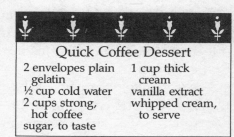

Quick Coffee Dessert

2 envelopes plain gelatin	1 cup thick cream
½ cup cold water	vanilla extract
2 cups strong, hot coffee	whipped cream, to serve
sugar, to taste	

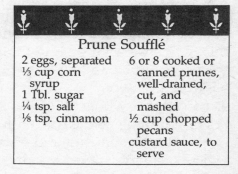

Prune Soufflé

2 eggs, separated	6 or 8 cooked or canned prunes, well-drained, cut, and mashed
⅓ cup corn syrup	
1 Tbl. sugar	
¼ tsp. salt	½ cup chopped pecans
⅛ tsp. cinnamon	custard sauce, to serve

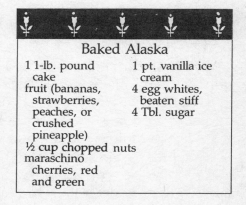

Baked Alaska

1 1-lb. pound cake	1 pt. vanilla ice cream
fruit (bananas, strawberries, peaches, or crushed pineapple)	4 egg whites, beaten stiff
	4 Tbl. sugar
½ cup chopped nuts	
maraschino cherries, red and green	

a ½-inch outside wall on each. Do not cut through the corners and do not cut all the way through to the bottom. Cake sides must remain attached to the base and to one another. Now that the middle section is detached on four sides, it must be cut away from the bottom to be removed. To do this, slip knife through one side of cake, ½-inch from bottom, and slide underneath middle section without cutting through corners or other three sides, and being sure to leave a ½-inch base. You should then be able to remove the center and have the hollowed-out cake remain standing. Place this on plate it is to be served from, but do not use your best, as it must go in the oven. Preheat oven to 500°.

Place a layer of fruit — bananas, strawberries, peaches, or crushed pineapple — on bottom. Sprinkle generously with ½ cup nuts. Then add maraschino cherries, both red and green, reserving 2 or 3 to decorate meringue. (Small bottles of cherries is what you want.) Have either homemade or store-bought vanilla ice cream (about a pint), and place this on fruit, packing tightly until cake is full. Then pack fruit, nuts, and cherries around the sides and over the top. Now put the first layer you cut off on top. Cover the whole cake (four sides and top) with a thick meringue, which should be already made (4 egg whites beaten stiff, and 4 Tbl. sugar). Place cake in 500° oven for about 4 minutes to brown meringue slightly. Whisk out, slice, and serve instantly! Serves 6.

We are so thrilled and excited over Dick's promotion. Think of his being a Captain! At this rate he'll be a General before the war is over! Tell him not to dare get another promotion, because being the mother of a Major would make me entirely too old! Well, Mrs. Captain, I salute you and anxiously await word that you are once more ensconsed in a home. Give Dick our love and tell him we are justly

proud of him. Don't hold your chin too high in the air — though I wouldn't blame you if you elevated it a little.

All love,
Mother

P.S. It seems I'm always bringing your chin into my letters, but after all a chin is a right important feature — and most expressive.

Atlanta, Georgia
November 10, 1942

Dear Selma:

Mothers have to be forgiven many weaknesses. I could not help being inordinately proud of your last letter. Of course I understood your homesickness. It's just as natural a thing as the leaves falling from the trees and skittering across the sidewalk. But looking it in the face and admitting that you are homesick has it already half whipped.

If the truth were known I'll wager that no bride who ever left her home town failed to be homesick sooner or later. The changing seasons bring with them those haunting, nostalgic memories, I think. Golden rod and aster growing by the roadside probably remind you of football season and all the things you used to do during that gay and carefree time. A cold winter night and you think of the times we gathered so cozily about the library fire, toasting marshmallows and roasting chestnuts in the coals. To this day, when in springtime I catch a whiff of locust trees in bloom, a wave of homesickness flows over me — a longing for Athens and the old home nestled in cedars and locust trees.

mama's house

Husbands can't understand why their brides aren't radiantly happy just to wait all day for their return home in the evenings. They can't know how lonely we sometimes get away from our family and friends, away from all familiar things. But you may be assured that you are not the only girl in the world who, having led a busy, exciting life at home, suddenly found herself in a strange new world, afflicted with homesickness.

You certainly have the right idea about it all, darling, and I'm too happy for words if, in cooking these familiar home foods, you have found a surcease to your longing for home. Cooking is a panacea for many moods. Not only are your hands occupied but your brain is busy and interested.

There is a homey comfort in the aromas that rise as the cooking goes on. Fragrances bring many associations of ideas and free the mind. So cook away, Selma — what if Dick does get fat as a pig!

You were an angel to send me the pound of coffee. I didn't know you didn't drink coffee. I gave Grandmother her pound. She said she was going to hide it from Bella and me to save for some great emergency. Perhaps she's wise because I consider every afternoon when I get home from the office a sufficient emergency to justify a cup of hot coffee!

I'm dead tonight — and my poor brain is paralyzed. We had our formal opening of the lounge for Wacs, Waves, and lady Marines this afternoon, and everything went off beautifully.

There was quite a distinquished gathering of uniforms — both male and female — but I had worked so hard to get the place attractive that the opening was really an anticlimax to me. I do hope the girls enjoy it, and they should as it is the only place in town exclusively for them.

Alice made some ice box cookies for you today. Bella has been very stingy with desserts lately, and I found out why just now when she asked me to address a package to you. Five pounds of sugar and ten pounds of pecans — now you can make a syrup pecan pie because Daddy ordered two quarts of syrup sent you from the farm. Better have hot cakes often too, so Dick can get his sugar by eating syrup.

Thanks a million for the two rare mustache cups. The lavender and gold one is the prize of my collection. I like "Egg In Sand" better than most old glass patterns, but that is probably because of my perverse nature. I've never seen an egg in sand because I've never been turtle hunting. *the beach*

The sketch of the old bridge with boat in dry dock was good. Vivid colors and done with a flair. But I love the ancient house! I feel I'd like to buy it and restore it to its former glory. There should be some quaint old waterfront shops that would make an interesting study.

Indeed I do think you should have guests for Thanksgiving. There is no better way to avoid feeling low than to be busy all day fixing a grand dinner for friends. Daddy thought a ham from the farm would start things off fine, so he's having one shipped to you today.

Be sure to use fruits as a centerpiece — piled in a pumpkin, you know — and make jack o'lanterns too.

Bella and I think the following menu would be nice:

MENU
Southern Baked Ham
Sweet Potatoes in Orange Cups
Asparagus Tips in Pepper Rings
Waldorf Salad in Apples
Jellied Cranberries
Celery and Olives
Hot Rolls
Mince Pie
Coffee

To prepare this **SOUTHERN BAKED HAM**, first scrub the country ham thoroughly with warm water and a stiff brush. Then boil 2-3 hours in a large roaster. Allow to cool. Place fat side up in an uncovered pan and bake in a 300° oven. A 10- to 12-lb. ham requires 25 minutes per pound; half hams require 30 minutes per pound. Remove from the oven 30 minutes before it is done, and cut off rind. Score fat in ¼-inch squares with sharp knife, spread with brown sugar, and sprinkle with allspice and cinnamon. Place a whole clove in the center of each square. Return to oven to finish cooking and to brown. Do not cook it in any of the syrups, ciders, or juices sometimes recommended. The ham would lose some of the delicious peanut flavor of a real South Georgia ham.

SWEET POTATOES IN ORANGE CUPS: Prepare

Southern Baked Ham

1 country ham	cinnamon
brown sugar	whole cloves
allspice	

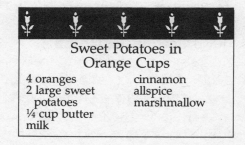

Sweet Potatoes in Orange Cups

4 oranges	cinnamon
2 large sweet	allspice
potatoes	marshmallow
¼ cup butter	
milk	

half an orange for each person. Cut oranges in half crosswise. Dig out pulp with a spoon, leaving orange peel whole. (Put pulp in ice box for tomorrow.) Boil and mash 2 large sweet potatoes (for 4 oranges). Add ¼ cup butter, a little milk, cinnamon, and allspice, and beat well. Fill orange cups full of mixture and top each with marshmallow. Run into oven to heat just before serving, but be sure to remove them just as the marshmallow puffs up and browns. Place these around the ham.

ASPARAGUS TIPS IN PEPPER RINGS: Select enough fairly large bell peppers to insure a large ring for each serving of asparagus. Cut peppers into ½-inch rings. Heat asparagus. Slip 5 or 6 stalks through a pepper ring until all is used. Place on platter and put strips of pimento over each end of asparagus. Have bowl of Hollandaise sauce (see pg. 15) conveniently placed beside platter.

WALDORF SALAD IN APPLES: Select 1 large red apple for each person. Cut off stem end. Using a spoon or apple corer, remove carefully all the pulp, leaving only enough to keep skins from breaking. With paring knife, remove all core and seeds from pulp and cut into small pieces. Add plenty of nuts and celery, mix well with mayonnaise, and fill apple cups to overflowing. Do you remember how we always stuck a tiny candle in each apple and had them all burning as Hutchins brought in the platter?

JELLIED CRANBERRIES: Pick over 1 lb. cranberries and wash. Use half as much sugar as berries (½ cup to 1 cup of berries) and half as much water as sugar. Put berries, sugar, and water in saucepan. Cover until berries begin to boil, then remove cover. Push berries under syrup (gently with a spoon so as not to break) until all are done. This requires about 10 minutes. Do not cook until the berries lose their shape or look dark. Pour into a pretty glass dish and cool. This will jell if 1 envelope gelatine soaked in 2 Tbl. cold water is added while fruit is hot. It makes a pretty mold, but we prefer it unmolded.

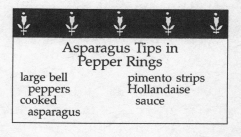

Asparagus Tips in Pepper Rings

large bell peppers	pimento strips
cooked asparagus	Hollandaise sauce

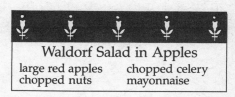

Waldorf Salad in Apples

large red apples	chopped celery
chopped nuts	mayonnaise

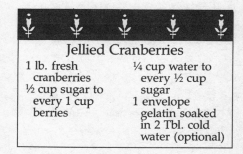

Jellied Cranberries

1 lb. fresh cranberries	¼ cup water to every ½ cup sugar
½ cup sugar to every 1 cup berries	1 envelope gelatin soaked in 2 Tbl. cold water (optional)

MINCE PIE: Make pie crust (see pg. 55). Line pie tin and set in ice box. Preheat oven to 350°. Chop 2 boxes prepared mincemeat into 4 cups water and put on to boil until water is absorbed. Add to this 1 cup chopped nuts, 2 cups chopped apple, 1 cup raisins, and ½ cup sherry. Put mixture into uncooked pie crust. Make crisscross strips across pie, sprinkle with sugar, dot with butter, and bake about 30 minutes. Top with whipped cream, ice cream, or a sliver of cheese. Oh boy, am I hungry! I can smell it now! Serves 6 to 8.

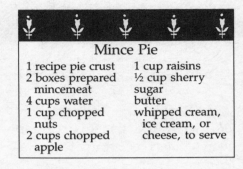

Mince Pie

1 recipe pie crust	1 cup raisins
2 boxes prepared mincemeat	½ cup sherry
4 cups water	sugar
1 cup chopped nuts	butter
2 cups chopped apple	whipped cream, ice cream, or cheese, to serve

If your Marines don't eat up all the ham, you might try Scalloped Ham, or scrambled eggs with chopped ham added, or Peppers Stuffed with Ham.

For **SCALLOPED HAM**, sprinkle bottom of buttered baking dish with bread crumbs, cover with a chopped hard-boiled egg and ½ cup white sauce, and then add a layer of chopped ham. Repeat. Cover top with bread crumbs. Bake in 350° oven until crumbs are brown (about 30 minutes).

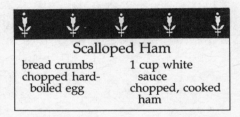

Scalloped Ham

bread crumbs	1 cup white sauce
chopped hard-boiled egg	chopped, cooked ham

PEPPERS STUFFED WITH HAM: Hollow out 2 bell peppers and boil until tender (about 5 minutes). Make 1 cup white sauce (see pg. 14), and add chopped ham, chopped pimentos, and sliced mushrooms. Fill hollowed-out peppers with mixture, sprinkle with bread crumbs, and bake at 350° for 15-20 minutes or until brown.

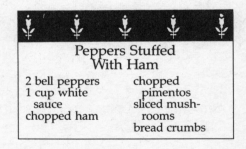

Peppers Stuffed With Ham

2 bell peppers	chopped pimentos
1 cup white sauce	sliced mushrooms
chopped ham	bread crumbs

CROQUETTES are a nice use of leftover meats. They are simple to make, provided you make them up early so the mixture can set before cooking. Almost any meat or fish will make excellent croquettes, and they may be made still more delicious by adding a cheese or tomato sauce, or with lamb or beef, a wine sauce. Here's a basic recipe:

BEEF CROQUETTES: Add 2 cups finely chopped, cooked meat and 1 Tbl. finely chopped onion to 1 cup thick white sauce (see pg. 14). Simmer this until onion is tender. Allow to get quite cold,

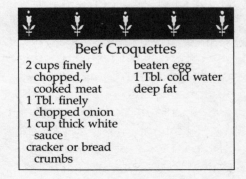

Beef Croquettes

2 cups finely chopped, cooked meat	beaten egg
1 Tbl. finely chopped onion	1 Tbl. cold water
1 cup thick white sauce	deep fat
cracker or bread crumbs	

then shape into rolls about three inches long or into balls. Roll in cracker or bread crumbs and then in beaten egg to which has been added 1 Tbl. cold water. Roll again in crumbs and fry in deep oil, dropping only about 3 at a time in the pan. Drain on brown paper. Serves 2 to 4. Chicken, turkey, lamb, veal, liver, fish, crab, shrimp, lobster, salmon, tuna, sweetbreads, brains — almost anything can be made into croquettes.

While you can get oysters in the shell do try our way of fixing them in imitation of those so famous at Antoine's in New Orleans. I don't know the secret of his and I never have that green, green seaweed he uses, but I have evolved some that are as good, if not better. Get the market man to show you how to open them — the right twist with a good stout knife and they are open. You'd best fix a dozen for Dick. I've seen Daddy eat two dozen!

OYSTERS ROCKEFELLER IMITATION: To begin with, fill 2 pie tins with ice cream salt (almost full) and put into the oven to get hot. Make a sauce of 1 small can (baby food size) strained spinach, 2 Tbl. butter, a dash of grated garlic, 1 Tbl. Worchestershire sauce, a dash of red pepper, 1 tsp. dry mustard, and the juice of ½ a lemon. Stir and beat this until very smooth, the consistency of Hollandaise. This makes enough sauce for 1 dozen oysters.

When salt is quite hot, remove from stove and arrange the half shells containing the oysters on the salt in a circle and in center if more than 8 are used. Cover each oyster solidly with sauce, and place under broiler until sauce is slightly browned and oyster hot through. Serve "as is" on pie pan on everyday platter.

For **POTATOES SUPREME**, select about 6 potatoes no larger than a hen's egg, and peel and slice crosswise in thin slices. Soak in water until a small frying pan (about 4 inches across) heats; melt 4 Tbl. butter in pan. Dry each potato slice on a towel and lay in bottom of pan slightly overlapping. Con-

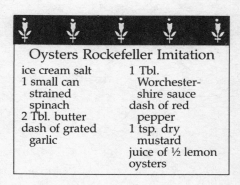

Oysters Rockefeller Imitation

ice cream salt	1 Tbl. Worchester-shire sauce
1 small can strained spinach	dash of red pepper
2 Tbl. butter	1 tsp. dry mustard
dash of grated garlic	juice of ½ lemon
	oysters

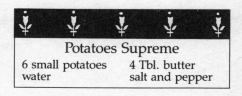

Potatoes Supreme

6 small potatoes	4 Tbl. butter
water	salt and pepper

tinue adding slices until all are used; salt and pepper each layer. Cover and cook over low heat about 20 minutes. Turn out onto plate as you would hoecake, without separating potatoes. These should be golden brown on bottom (which becomes top) and cooked well through. Dick will want these often, so practice a bit. Serves 2.

CHERRY POINT SEAFOOD: While you are so near that grand seafood market at Morehead City, do have this main dish often. I'm sending you a set of shells to serve it in but if they are delayed, just put it in ramekins or baking dishes or pile on toast. You can't miss!

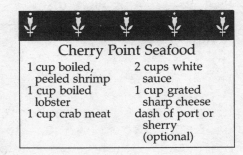

Cherry Point Seafood

1 cup boiled, peeled shrimp	2 cups white sauce
1 cup boiled lobster	1 cup grated sharp cheese
1 cup crab meat	dash of port or sherry (optional)

Mix 1 cup of boiled, peeled shrimp, 1 cup boiled lobster, and 1 cup crab meat with 2 cups white sauce (see pg. 14) to which has been added 1 cup grated sharp cheese. Run under flame to brown if used in shells or baking dish. I add a dash of port or sherry if I feel in a festive mood. Serves 6.

Daddy leaves tomorrow for points east, to be gone a week. He's much too busy and has so many people to advise and help, now that so many men are gone. I often think that those too old to go are heavily overburdened at home — minus the dangers of combat, of course — but even so the tired businessman of today is an unsung soldier.

With love,
Mother

Atlanta, Georgia
December 10, 1942

Dear Selma:

I don't blame you for feeling smug and egotistical; such an accomplishment as Christmas gifts already bought and wrapped fully justifies it! Gracious me, I haven't given a thought to the matter. Stewart and Alice have already told me what they want — and Bella wants a brass lamp! My list is longer every year. This year I will have to limit it mainly to young folks.

So glad you feel that since the Thanksgiving dinner went off so well you can have a Christmas dinner for some of the lonesome Marines whose wives are so far away. Christmas is an emotional, spiritual season. The knowledge that you and Dick are giving untold pleasure to your homesick fellows will put you both in the proper frame of mind, and I'll bet my shiniest dime you'll be so busy and happy on Christmas day you won't have time for a thought of us. But do waft us one little tiny thought. I'll have to bring in some lonesome fellows too to liven up so much family. As usual, the family will all have dinner here.

Dick is going to be the worst spoiled Marine that ever left this country!! C rations are going to be hard to take after all the good things he's had at home. The news of his working to get a fighter squadron ready to leave does not warm my heart, but sends cold chills down my spine. *C'est le guerre* is much too trite to use, though perhaps to borrow that favorite phrase from the French is about as good a way to sum it up as any. Sometimes in my quiet moments I wonder how we find life livable — but we not only find it livable but exciting and interesting. For fortunately the human spirit was given fortitude and resiliency.

Going in groups to the curb market at Morehead City in the "dawn's early light" sounds much too energetic for an old housekeeper, but just goes to prove what I've always said — that this generation of young people has what it takes!

Now let's get down to the Christmas dinner. Here is a suggested menu:

MENU
Eggnog or Milk Punch
Christmas Turkey
Atlanta Turkey Stuffing
Cranberry Sauce
Vegetables
Relish Tray
Toasted Rolls
Grapefruit Baskets of Ambrosia
Coffee

Turkey is a must. I tried having a big hen once when we were young and hard up, but never again. It just wasn't any fun, in spite of everything I did to spice it up. Ever since then, I start hiding money for a **CHRISTMAS TURKEY** early in the fall.

I figure they are not much more in the end because you always have enough left for sandwiches, and one dish of creamed turkey, and one turkey hash and waffle breakfast, and grand dressing heated up, and then soup from the bones! Heavens, what do you want for your money?

Be sure and go to a good market. And do not be satisfied with any but the finest quality bird, regardless of the few cents difference in price. Your whole day of work is wasted unless you get a first class turkey, because no amount of "fixins" will change a bad old stringy bird into a luscious *pièce de résistance* for your Christmas dinner. So I repeat — get a good turkey. The size will depend upon the size of your oven and the price you want to pay. Allow 1 lb. for each person for dinner, 4 lbs. for the carcass and as many lbs. for leftovers as possible. I think if you can find a plump, 12-lb. hen, you will be fixed for 8 people.

Serve milk punches before dinner in place of egg-nog, unless, of course, you can find whipping cream

and Dick will make the eggnog. Since you will have to use buffet style, omit a first course and have a green vegetable (green peas or broccoli), beets or cauliflower (unless you have broccoli), and a generous sized bowl of celery sticks, carrot curls, and olives. Include cranberry sauce, of course, and have juicy red sauce, not dark jelly! Top this off with ambrosia in grapefruit baskets. I think bread is flexible — you could have dinner rolls, but I believe I'd just get bakery rolls, and split, butter, and toast them. Even light bread will be sufficient, because with dressing and rice, very little bread will be needed.

I'm sure by now you're an expert at vegetable dishes so I'll skip those and tell you how to fix your turkey: Place turkey in pan of water; scrub skin well; rinse and dry. Pick off any stray pin feathers and tie legs securely together. Turkey is now ready to chill. When stuffing: Fill opening where neck was removed with stuffing, being careful not to crowd, as room must be left for swelling. Secure with metal skewer or sew together. Salt and lightly stuff large cavity and secure in a similar fashion.

ATLANTA TURKEY STUFFING: Bake a deep frying pan of egg bread (see below). Break bread into pieces. Add 6 slices of white bread and any cold biscuits you have on hand. Over this, pour 1 qt. sweet milk. Chop a stalk of celery fine, chop 2 onions, and mix with bread. Break 6 whole eggs into this and add 2 Tbl. poultry seasoning. Now melt ½ lb. butter or margarine and mix in well with dressing. Salt and pepper to taste. The dressing should be thick — if not, add more bread. If you desire you may add a pound of sausage or a pound of boiled, peeled chestnuts. Daddy prefers it with a quart of oysters. Fill a baking pan with any leftover dressing and cook in oven at 350° for about 30 minutes.

After turkey is stuffed, make a **TURKEY CRUST** — a thick dough of 6 cups flour, 1 tsp. salt, 1 cup shortening, and enough cold water for a *very* stiff

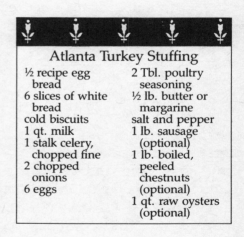

Atlanta Turkey Stuffing

½ recipe egg bread	2 Tbl. poultry seasoning
6 slices of white bread	½ lb. butter or margarine
cold biscuits	salt and pepper
1 qt. milk	1 lb. sausage (optional)
1 stalk celery, chopped fine	1 lb. boiled, peeled chestnuts (optional)
2 chopped onions	
6 eggs	1 qt. raw oysters (optional)

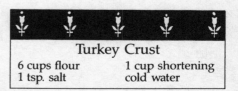

Turkey Crust

6 cups flour	1 cup shortening
1 tsp. salt	cold water

dough. Roll out about 1-inch thick. Grease bird well with shortening and cover thickly with the dough, pressing it firmly into place. Put on in roasting pan in oven and bake for about 4 hours at 350°. This method eliminates basting and assures tenderness. Do not remove crust until turkey is out of stove. To test for doneness, stick a fork in the part of wing joint adjoining the body. If tender, it is done.

EGG BREAD: Beat together 4 eggs until light. Add 4 cups buttermilk, 6 Tbl. melted shortening, and 3 tsp. salt. Add 4 cups corn meal and beat smooth. Sift in 4 tsp. baking powder, and dissolve 2 tsp. baking soda in spoon of water and add to batter last. Melt shortening in 9-inch iron skillet and then pour batter into greasy skillet. Bake in preheated 450° oven, 20 minutes.

To make **GRAPEFRUIT BASKETS**, cut 4 grapefruits in half, scoop out pulp and, discard seeds and membrane. (Reserve pulp for ambrosia.) Make your cups look festive by sticking (with toothpick) a sprig of holly or mistletoe on either side. Flute edges of cup with knife. Makes 8 baskets.

AMBROSIA: Open a fresh coconut by hitting hard with a hammer. Put halves into a hot oven a few minutes to loosen meat from shell. Cut off brown skin and grate the meat. (Or you can use canned coconut.) Peel 8 oranges (1 per person) and remove membrane, discarding core and seeds. Slice pulp lengthways. Cut into halves 2 lbs. Malaga or Tokay grapes and remove seeds. Mix with orange slices and grapefruit and blend in the grated coconut. Sprinkle with sugar and fill grapefruit bakets.

For **EGGNOG**, beat 12 egg yolks. Add 12 Tbl. sugar and 12 Tbl. good whiskey, putting in an extra 1 or 2 of the whiskey for good measure. Let set while you whip the 12 egg whites until stiff. Fold these into 1 pt. heavy cream which has been whipped; then fold in yellow mixture until all is mixed. Serves 16 to 20.

MILK PUNCH: To 1 cup whole milk add 2 tsp.

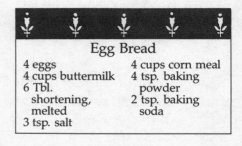

Egg Bread

4 eggs	4 cups corn meal
4 cups buttermilk	4 tsp. baking powder
6 Tbl. shortening, melted	2 tsp. baking soda
3 tsp. salt	

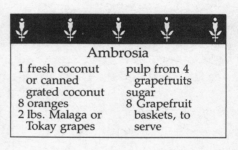

Ambrosia

1 fresh coconut or canned grated coconut	pulp from 4 grapefruits
8 oranges	sugar
2 lbs. Malaga or Tokay grapes	8 Grapefruit baskets, to serve

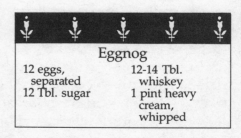

Eggnog

12 eggs, separated	12-14 Tbl. whiskey
12 Tbl. sugar	1 pint heavy cream, whipped

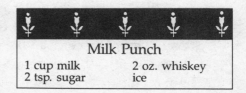

Milk Punch

1 cup milk	2 oz. whiskey
2 tsp. sugar	ice

sugar and 2 oz. whiskey. Shake in milk shaker or in quart milk bottle until foamy. Pour over ice cubes and serve. Serves 2.

A tiny, lighted Christmas tree would be an exciting centerpiece for your dinner. Maybe the dime store will have miniature Santas and sleighs and deer, or a jumble of toys which may be presented to the guests for their amusement after dinner.

Since your Christmas gifts are all wrapped for mailing, you will have time to make some candy, provided sugar holds out. These two require very little sugar and are delicious.

PEANUT BRITTLE: Use 1 cup sugar and ¾ cup peanuts, chopped or halved. Put nuts on buttered plate and set on stove to warm. Melt sugar, stirring constantly until brown. If porous candy is desired, add ¼ tsp. baking soda when sugar is brown. When golden brown, pour over nuts on buttered dish. Break up when cold.

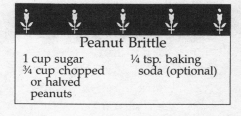

Peanut Brittle	
1 cup sugar	¼ tsp. baking
¾ cup chopped	soda (optional)
or halved	
peanuts	

PANOCHE: Use 1 cup light brown sugar, ½ cup white sugar, and 6 Tbl. sweet milk. Boil together until mixture forms a soft ball. Add ½ tsp. butter and cool. When cool, add ½ tsp. vanilla extract and ½ cup chopped nuts. Beat until thick and creamy. Turn out in buttered dish or pan. When dry on surface, cut into squares.

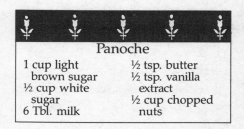

Panoche	
1 cup light	½ tsp. butter
brown sugar	½ tsp. vanilla
½ cup white	extract
sugar	½ cup chopped
6 Tbl. milk	nuts

For lunch the day after Christmas, treat Dick to a **TURKEY EGG BREAD SANDWICH**. (Use ¼ recipe for egg bread on pg. 108.) Cut bread into 4-inch squares, and split through the middle. Cover lower slice with turkey, put on top slice, and pour over this plenty of hot gravy (see pg. 17) made from stock saved from Christmas dinner. This good plebeian food tastes wonderful after a feast the day before.

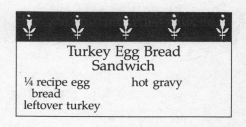

Turkey Egg Bread Sandwich	
¼ recipe egg	hot gravy
bread	
leftover turkey	

So glad you found bittersweet (semi-sweet) chocolate in the Commissary. I thought it was extinct! So here's the **BITTERSWEET ICE CREAM** recipe. Whip 1 pt. cream stiff. Melt ½ lb. bittersweet chocolate. Fold chocolate into whipped cream, put in pan, and freeze 2 hours. Lucky you! Serves 4.

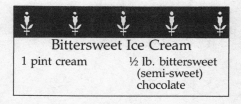

Bittersweet Ice Cream	
1 pint cream	½ lb. bittersweet
	(semi-sweet)
	chocolate

Since you can get such grand ice cream in bulk, why not search Beaufort stores next time you are there for marrons and have them on the ice cream? Or, for a **FROZEN CRÈME DE MENTHE PARFAIT** get a bottle of crème de menthe and freeze slightly in ice box. Use parfait glasses if the house furnishes them, water glasses if not, and put in a dip of vanilla ice cream. Pour over some of the half-frozen crème de menthe, add more ice cream, and top off with crème de menthe. This is "out of this world" as Alice says.

Frozen Crème de
Menthe Parfait

1 bottle crème de menthe	vanilla ice cream

Little Alice is all excited about you being on a huge Marine air station, where aviators will be a dime a dozen, and if it were not for school, I fear you would have a visitor, young though she is.

This has been a very busy day and Daddy's birthday to boot. I had Julia and Bob, and Edith and Will to dinner and he felt nicely celebrated. Tomorrow is Grandmother's birthday and I have no idea what can be done for her pleasure. We seem to be having our birthdays all in a bunch.

Stewart has orders to report to Parris Island on Jan. 5th for boot training. Can you believe he's old enough to go to war?

Lots of love,
Mother

P.S. Bella has baked you a white fruit cake, so I am including a bottle of wine. This will be handy when guests drop in.

Atlanta, Georgia
January 1, 1943

My darling child:

Tomorrow is your birthday, and I'm being shamelessly sentimental remembering the wonderful times we've had getting ready for parties. Remember the one when you were ten years old and we made paper flower holders for the ice cream and nuts, and had the huge paper flower grab bag? Fifty came that time and it was so lovely on the lawn under the tall pines.

I think if war does no other good, it makes us realize how important it is for a child — for all children — to have a happy childhood. I have so many precious memories stored away and I enjoy bringing them out one by one to live over again.

I fear I shall have to depend more and more on memories now that Stewart has gone. I regret so much that he had to miss his senior year in high school due to that year he was so ill and had to stay out of school. Oh well, all life is uncertain and Fate plays a large part. I'm sure he'll make a fine Marine and I'm so proud of him!

I seem to have drifted far from your birthday — congratulations upon your twenty-third, my dear. It's a wonderful age to be. (Any age is.) Who was it said "Youth is such a wonderful thing to waste on young people?" It's true that we cannot appreciate our blessings fully while we have them. I often think "blessings brighten as they take their flight," but what of it? Life grows richer every day and new beauties come to each of us. So why worry if we can't still look sixteen and capture every man we meet?

The only complaint I have with growing older is that my feet hurt. (Mama says a lady can say her foot hurts and still be a lady, but no lady would say her *feet* hurt.) That's right in line with lots of Mama's maxims. Another one is that a real lady can cross a muddy street without getting mud on her shoes!

Well, I ask you — does she go barefooted? Has Mama ever tried Georgia's red clay?

Back to the birthday — I'm sending you a pretty spring dress in which I feel sure you will dazzle the respected citizens of New Bern. Tell Dick I selected red because that is his favorite color on you. Is that being a diplomatic Mama?

Have a wonderful birthday and know that Daddy and I are remembering all the joy you have brought us through these happy years.

> Count your garden by the flowers,
>   Never by the leaves that fall;
> Count your days by golden hours,
>   Don't remember clouds at all;
> Count your night by stars, not shadows;
> Count your life by smiles, not tears;
> And to bring you joy this birthday,
> Count your age by *friends*, not years.

So, your friends want to taste some real southern-style barbecue and Brunswick stew. Well, I wish they could taste some that is really-truly southern-style barbecue and honest-to-goodness Brunswick stew, but that is out of the question because you could not find the hickory and pecan wood to cook with even if you had an iron pot. A situation which reminds me of the old fellow who, having been handed out two slices of bread and butter said, "Lady, I'd have a ham and egg sandwich if I had some ham, provided I had an egg."

So for barbecue and Brunswick stew, you know the main ingredient of these two succulent viands is the *smoke*. Smoke from seasoned pecan and hickory wood that mixes and mingles with the savory sauces for about twelve hours until it is part and parcel of the whole. And then I feel sure an acorn or two drop into the pot from the old oak tree overhead, and perhaps a leaf or two. Then there's a bit of sunshine

and a balmy breeze thrown in for good measure —
and a blue sky. That is absolutely indispensable!

But if you want to contrive some minus these
main ingredients, I think you may do so quite suc-
cessfully as I doubt if the "damn-Yankees" would
know the difference. For 12 people, buy a small pork
shoulder, 2 large lamb shoulders with the ribs on, a
nice fat hen, 4 cans Shoe Peg corn, 3 No. 2 cans
tomatoes (it's a good thing everybody's chipping in),
and 6 onions. If lamb is scarce, use beef, or all pork.

Now, for the **BARBECUE**: Beg or borrow the
largest turkey roaster on the base and a large pot
with cover. Buy everything the day before, and as
soon as Dick leaves the next morning, skin and wash
the 2 lamb shoulders and put them in the turkey
roaster with about 3 inches of water. Pour over this a
sauce made of 1 bottle Worchestershire sauce, 4 Tbl.
mustard, 1 cup vinegar, 1 cup sugar, 1 Tbl. salt, 1 tsp.
black pepper, 1 10-oz. bottle catsup, 1 1¼-oz. box chili
powder, and 4 Tbl. flour. Mix together and pour over
lamb. Cook in 400° oven, covered, until water and
lamb are hot; lower to 300° and let remain covered
for about 2 hours. Remove cover, turn meat, and
cook until meat is so tender it will fall off bones and
is browned. The sauce should be *dark* red and thick
like gravy by now. Don't try to carve this. Just serve
it in chunks. If this is ready long before serving time,
so much the better. The longer it stays in the sauce
the more it will taste like real barbecue. Just reheat.

BRUNSWICK STEW: Put chicken and pork in
large pot. Open 3 cans tomatoes, pour over chicken
and pork, and add enough water to cover meat and 6
onions, chopped. Put in the juice of 2 lemons, 1 bay
leaf, 2 tsp. salt, and 1 Tbl. sugar. Cover and let
simmer for 2-3 hours, adding more water if necessary. When the meat falls off the chicken, remove it
and take all meat off the bones and return meat to
kettle. Do the same with the pork. Cover and let
simmer 2 hours more until the meat is just a pulpy
mass. This requires frequent stirring, so as to shred

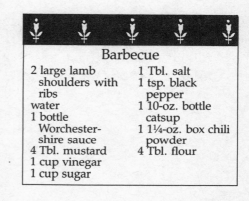

Barbecue

2 large lamb shoulders with ribs	1 Tbl. salt
	1 tsp. black pepper
water	1 10-oz. bottle catsup
1 bottle Worchester-shire sauce	1 1¼-oz. box chili powder
4 Tbl. mustard	4 Tbl. flour
1 cup vinegar	
1 cup sugar	

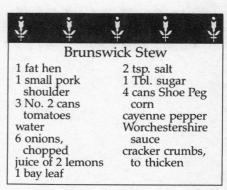

Brunswick Stew

1 fat hen	2 tsp. salt
1 small pork shoulder	1 Tbl. sugar
3 No. 2 cans tomatoes	4 cans Shoe Peg corn
water	cayenne pepper
6 onions, chopped	Worchestershire sauce
juice of 2 lemons	cracker crumbs, to thicken
1 bay leaf	

the meat and prevent sticking. Now add the canned corn and some cayenne pepper. Continue cooking over lowest heat until dark brown and thick, but stir to prevent scorching. Skim off fat as it rises to the top. Taste, and add more salt, hot pepper, and Worchestershire sauce if needed. Thicken with cracker crumbs, if necessary. This is an all day job. Don't plan to get your hair set this day!

Make a tart cold slaw to go with it, and have plenty of dill pickles, sliced tomatoes, sliced bread, and hot coffee or cold beer, depending upon the preferences of your guests. This should make a quite acceptable repast and I hope you have fun fixing it with your new friends.

> With love,
> Mother

Atlanta, Georgia
February 12, 1943

Selma darling:

Such wonderful news! I've simply been walking on air ever since your letter came saying you and Dick would get a furlough, and I've asked for time off for the duration of your visit. If I was doing work for which I received compensation, I'd no doubt get a holiday but since it's "volunteer" work I'll probably have to go right on packing clothes for the Russians and rope you and Dick in to help.

Never mind — it's too good to be true that you'll actually be here. It will help me to forget that Stewart's ten day furlough is over and he's gone to New River for advanced training. I'm happy for him, and proud that I have so fine a son, but . . . .

Bella is on her toes getting ready for your arrival, and if the fatted calf isn't killed it won't be her fault.

Why, oh why, do you want the recipe for Blueberry Roll when you are coming home so soon? They do grow marvelous blueberries there, but serve them with cream and sugar — I haven't time to do a recipe — besides I'm too excited.

Of course I'll keep the cherry table. Have you any idea where you'll go next?

I'm glad you'll be forced to eat at the Officer's Club after your things leave — you've taken cooking much too seriously. Besides, it should be so delightful to eat in a setting of sailboats on a river bend.

Love,
Mother

P.S. Bella, feeling sorry for you, came forward and asked me to enclose this.

BELLA'S BLUEBERRY COBBLER recipe —
Little Lady: Make a rich pie crust (see pg. 55). Roll it thin as a razor blade. Cut in strips and lay

Bella's Blueberry Cobbler
½ recipe pie	butter
pastry	½ cup cold water
blueberries	
sugar	

some in bottom of deep casserole. Cover with blueberries. Sprinkle with sugar and dot with butter.
Add more strips, berries, sugar, and butter. Add a
top layer of pastry strips, sugar, and butter. Pour ½
cup cold water over all and bake 45 minutes at 350°.
This is the way Mrs. W. taught me and Mr. W. says it
is the best ever.

Love,
Bella

Atlanta, Georgia
March 3, 1943

Selma darling:

The past ten days have been like a year while waiting to hear of your safe arrival at Eagle Mountain Lake, Texas.

Old Matilda the Faithful must indeed be made of stern stuff to carry you and Dick such distances with no grumbling. I visualized punctures and engine trouble all the way, which only goes to prove that most of our troubles are imagined ones.

Here at home we've settled down to a *low* low since you left. The furlough was all too short and while we enjoyed every moment you were here, it only intensified our loneliness when you left. But these are not times to waste worrying or grieving over what is to be, so I try to picture you and Dick enjoying new scenery as you speed along to new adventures.

Weren't you lucky to find so many of your old friends at home? Young people certainly keep on the move these days. We seem to have turned into a nation of gypsies overnight, and I marvel at the ease and good humor with which it is done.

Both you and Dick looked simply wonderful, all of which reflects happy hearts and that you are taking good care of each other. I shall have many happy memories stored away for my pleasure until you come again.

You two must lead a charmed life! Except for New Bern, you have been so lucky in all of your house-hunting forays. What could be nicer than a lakeside cabin with a huge, stone fireplace for chilly evenings. That sounds almost too good to be true.

You are going to have such fun. I've heard that Eagle Mountain Lake is full of wonderful fat bass and perch. I can almost smell them frying now! I do

hope you will have an outdoor **FISH FRY AND CORN ROAST** (when corn comes in). There is nothing so much fun.

First, catch your fish! Scale them, cut off heads, split down one side, and clean. Wash thoroughly and put on ice until time for the party to begin.

Get enough corn (yellow Bantam if possible) for each guest to have plenty — 2 ears a person probably. And make up a big bowl of hush puppies.

Build a rock or brick stand about 1½ ft. high to hold a rack from your oven. Use that as the stove for your skillet. Lay a good fire under this and have a separate fire if you like for your corn roasting. Let fire for corn burn down to hot embers and then push the unshucked roasting ears under the coals near the ground. Let roast about 30 minutes.

FRIED FISH: When the fire under the rack is hot, put your skillet on rack and fill with about 1 inch of cooking oil or bacon drippings. In the meantime, salt and pepper your fish and dip in corn meal. When the fat is hot, put fish in pan and fry until brown and crisp, turning when necessary. To make delectable **HUSH PUPPIES**, make a very thick hoecake batter (see pg. 38) by adding less water than you would for hoecakes. Drop batter by spoonfuls into hot oil while your fish is frying. Keep fire hot until all fish and hush-puppies have finished cooking.

By the time dinner is ready, your guests will be starving and the food will disappear like magic. You can even toast marshmallows over the coals for dessert. Everybody likes an outdoor dinner so get ready and go fishing!

Here are the Mexican recipes you asked for. Inez sent them from San Antonio and they are excellent, and Texas is the proper locale for them.

For **TORTILLAS AMERICANA**, use 1 cup corn meal, 1 cup boiling water, 1 tsp. salt, and 2 tsp. bacon

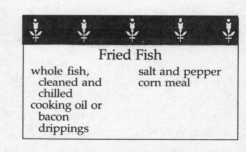

Fried Fish

whole fish, cleaned and chilled	salt and pepper corn meal
cooking oil or bacon drippings	

Hush Puppies

thick hoecake batter	hot oil

Tortillas Americana

1 cup boiling water	1 tsp. salt
1 cup corn meal	2 tsp. bacon drippings

drippings. Stir the boiling water into the corn meal, add salt and bacon drippings, and mix well. Pat into thin, flat cakes and bake on ungreased or very slightly greased griddle, turning as they brown. This makes about 24 tortillas.

For **ENCHILADAS**, use 18 tortillas (buy these — they have to be very thin), ½ cup cooking oil, ½ cup grated cheese, 1 onion, sliced, ½ tsp. salt, 1 No. 2 can of Gebhardt's chili con carne, and ½ tsp. Gebhardt's chili powder. Heat tortillas in hot oil (1 second on each side), spread with chili con carne, and roll. Stack the rolls parallel to each other on a hot platter and pour over them the rest of the chili. Sprinkle with grated sharp cheese and run in 350° oven to heat. Top with thinly-sliced onion, a little salt, and a dash of chili powder. Serve at once. Serves 6.

TAMAL DE POLLO (Chicken Tamale Pie): Assemble 1 can Gebhardt's tamales, 1 can tomato purée, 1 can corn, 1 cup chopped ripe olives, ¼ cup raisins, 1 tsp. salt, 2 tsp. chili powder, 2 cups cooked chicken, 1 cup broth or gravy, and ½ cup grated sharp cheese. Slice 8 Tamales (1 can) and line a ½-qt. casserole. Mix other ingredients and pour into casserole. Sprinkle with cheese and bake in 350° oven for 1 hour. Serves 6.

CAMARON ESTILO LOUISIANA: Assemble 2 cups cooked, peeled shrimp, 1 Tbl. butter, 1 tsp. minced onion, 4 Tbl. flour, 1 tsp. salt, 1 tsp. chili powder, 2 cups milk, 2 Tbl. minced parsley, 4 Tbl. catsup. Cook onion in butter until soft. Add shrimp which have been broken into pieces. Brown. Stir in flour, salt, chili powder, and then gradually, the milk. Cook 5 minutes. Add catsup and parsley. Cover and steam for several minutes. Serve over hot rice or toast. Serves 4.

For **FRITADA DE POLLO**, use a 3-lb. chicken; ½ cup flour; ½ cup oil; 1 onion, sliced; 1 green pepper, chopped; 2 cloves garlic, minced; 4 Tbl. catsup; 1 cup water; 1 tsp. chili powder; 1 cup sherry or claret; 1 tsp. salt; 4 Tbl. raisins; 8 ripe olives, chopped; and 2 cups

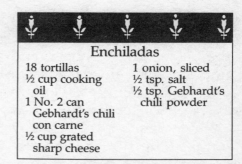

Enchiladas

18 tortillas	1 onion, sliced
½ cup cooking oil	½ tsp. salt
1 No. 2 can Gebhardt's chili con carne	½ tsp. Gebhardt's chili powder
½ cup grated sharp cheese	

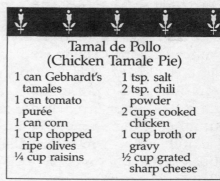

Tamal de Pollo (Chicken Tamale Pie)

1 can Gebhardt's tamales	1 tsp. salt
1 can tomato purée	2 tsp. chili powder
1 can corn	2 cups cooked chicken
1 cup chopped ripe olives	1 cup broth or gravy
¼ cup raisins	½ cup grated sharp cheese

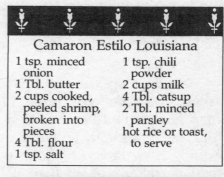

Camaron Estilo Louisiana

1 tsp. minced onion	1 tsp. chili powder
1 Tbl. butter	2 cups milk
2 cups cooked, peeled shrimp, broken into pieces	4 Tbl. catsup
	2 Tbl. minced parsley
4 Tbl. flour	hot rice or toast, to serve
1 tsp. salt	

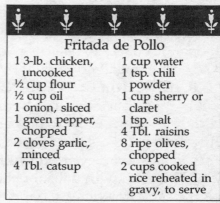

Fritada de Pollo

1 3-lb. chicken, uncooked	1 cup water
½ cup flour	1 tsp. chili powder
½ cup oil	1 cup sherry or claret
1 onion, sliced	1 tsp. salt
1 green pepper, chopped	4 Tbl. raisins
2 cloves garlic, minced	8 ripe olives, chopped
4 Tbl. catsup	2 cups cooked rice reheated in gravy, to serve

cooked rice. Cut up chicken, dip in flour, and brown in hot oil. Remove chicken to large skillet. Simmer the onion, green pepper, and garlic in the hot oil until brown. Add catsup, water, and chili powder and boil 5 minutes. Pour over chicken, adding sherry and salt, and water as needed. Cover and allow to simmer until chicken is tender (about 1½ hours). Fifteen minutes before serving, add raisins and ripe olives. Reheat rice in the gravy and serve around chicken on platter. Serves 6.

COSTILLAS RELLENAS: Assemble 2 Tbl. minced onion, 4 Tbl. melted butter, 1 cup stale bread crumbs, ½ tsp. salt, ½ tsp. chili powder, milk to moisten, and 6 pork chops cut for stuffing. Cook onion in butter until tender; add crumbs and continue cooking until brown. Add seasonings and enough milk to moisten. Use chops about 1-inch thick. From the meat side, make a pocket and fill with the stuffing. Secure edges with toothpicks. Bake in 350° oven about 40 minutes or until tender. Serves 6.

For **TORTA DE CARNE ENCHILADA**, use 2 lbs. beef, 1 onion, 2 slices stale toast, 1 egg, 2 tomatoes (fresh or canned), 2 tsp. salt, and 2 tsp. chili powder. Put beef, onion, and stale toast through food chopper (or have meat ground twice at butcher's). Mix other ingredients into beef thoroughly and form into oblong loaf, adding additional crumbs or liquid as needed to bind loaf together. Dredge with flour. Heat 4 Tbl. oil in small roaster, add loaf, and turn so that it will brown on all sides. When brown, pour over ½ cup tomato juice and enough hot water to half cover loaf. Cover and bake in 350° oven 1 hour. Serves 8.

QUICK CHILI CON CARNE: Place a No. 2 can of Gebhardt's chili con carne in a sauce pan and cover with hot water. Allow to boil gently for 20 minutes. Turn into hot bowls and serve at once. Serves 2.

To make your own **HOMEMADE CHILI CON CARNE**, start with 2 lbs. of beef. (Cheaper cuts are permissable for this.) Chop or cut into very small

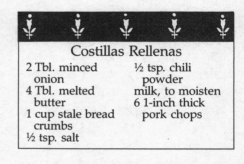

Costillas Rellenas

2 Tbl. minced onion	½ tsp. chili powder
4 Tbl. melted butter	milk, to moisten
1 cup stale bread crumbs	6 1-inch thick pork chops
½ tsp. salt	

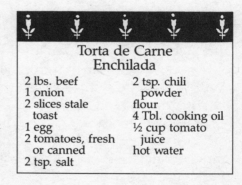

Torta de Carne Enchilada

2 lbs. beef	2 tsp. chili powder
1 onion	flour
2 slices stale toast	4 Tbl. cooking oil
1 egg	½ cup tomato juice
2 tomatoes, fresh or canned	hot water
2 tsp. salt	

Homemade Chili con Carne

2 lbs. beef	1 onion, chopped
2 Tbl. chili powder	2 tsp. salt
2 cloves garlic, minced	1½ qts. hot water
3 Tbl. flour	2 cans Mexican-style beans
4 Tbl. fat	

chunks, but don't grind. Mix with 2 Tbl. chili powder, 2 cloves garlic, minced, and 3 Tbl. flour. Melt 4 Tbl. fat in a large, deep pot and simmer chopped onion until tender, before adding the meat mixture. Cook 10 minutes or until brown. Add 2 tsp. salt and gradually pour on 1½ qts. hot water. Simmer 45 minutes or until meat is tender. Then add 2 cans Mexican-style beans and heat thoroughly before serving. Serves 8-10.

For **HUEVOS COCIDOS EN ARROZ**, preheat oven to 350°. Wash 6 Tbl. uncooked rice, dry well, and brown with 1 large onion (chopped) in 2 Tbl. butter. Add 1½ cups beef broth, ½ tsp. salt, and ½ tsp. chili powder. Mix well. Turn into a buttered casserole, cover, and bake at 350° until rice is almost tender (about 40 minutes). Uncover; make 6 indentations in the rice and break into these 6 whole eggs. Sprinkle with grated sharp cheese, salt, and more chili powder, if desired. Continue baking until eggs are set and cheese is melted (about 10 minutes). Serves 6.

CHILI CON CARNE Y HUEVOS: Fry 2 eggs. Heat 1 can prepared chili and turn into a hot serving dish. Top with the fried eggs and garnish with watercress or lettuce, and radish roses. Serves 2.

MEXICAN RICE: Brown 3 cups cooked rice in 4 Tbl. hot fat. Season with 1 tsp. salt and 1 tsp. chili powder. Turn it into a hot serving dish and pour over it 1 cup chili sauce. Sprinkle with grated sharp cheese, lifting rice with fork so that cheese may coat each grain. Serve hot. Serves 6 to 8.

POLLO EN PARRILLAS CON SALSA BARBACOA: Split a small broiling chicken down the back and brush with melted butter. Sear under hot broiler flame. Reduce flame and continue cooking about 15 minutes. Brush with barbecue sauce and turn over twice during the cooking to brown evenly. Serve with extra barbecue sauce. To make **BARBECUE SAUCE**, combine in sauce pan ¼ cup vinegar, 1 cup catsup, 1 cup red wine, 2 Tbl. brown

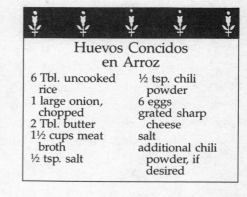

Huevos Concidos en Arroz

6 Tbl. uncooked rice	½ tsp. chili powder
1 large onion, chopped	6 eggs
2 Tbl. butter	grated sharp cheese
1½ cups meat broth	salt
½ tsp. salt	additional chili powder, if desired

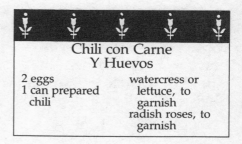

Chili con Carne Y Huevos

2 eggs	watercress or lettuce, to garnish
1 can prepared chili	radish roses, to garnish

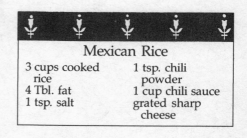

Mexican Rice

3 cups cooked rice	1 tsp. chili powder
4 Tbl. fat	1 cup chili sauce
1 tsp. salt	grated sharp cheese

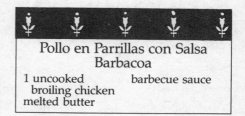

Pollo en Parrillas con Salsa Barbacoa

1 uncooked broiling chicken	barbecue sauce
melted butter	

sugar, 1 tsp. dry mustard, 1 tsp. paprika, 1 tsp. red pepper, 1 onion (chopped), 1 clove garlic (chopped), 2 Tbl. Worchestershire sauce, and 2 Tbl. butter. Simmer 30 minutes. Serves 2.

For **HUEVOS ENDIABLADOS EN ASPIC**, dissolve 3 bouillon cubes and 1 package lemon gelatin in 1 cup hot water. Add ½ cup cold water, ½ cup tomato juice, 1 tsp. minced onion and, ¼ tsp. salt. Pour a thin layer of gelatin mixture in bottom of 1 large round mold or 6 individual molds, and place in ice box until firm. Chill remaining gelatin until thick, but not firm. Sprinkle the firm gelatin with chili powder and arrange 6 devilled egg halves (see pg. 54) over it. Cover with a thin layer of gelatin, a layer of cooked green peas, another layer of gelatin, and a layer of cooked and sliced carrots, and fill mold with remaining gelatin. Chill until firm and serve on lettuce with mayonnaise. Serves 6.

ENSALADA ESTILO SOMBRERO: Season 2 cups cottage cheese with 1 tsp. salt, ½ tsp. chili powder, and enough pineapple juice to moisten (about ½ cup or less). Mold into cones about 2 inches in diameter. Place a cone on each slice of pineapple, and either leave peaked or crease to represent the sombrero. At the base of each, arrange strips of green pepper for the hat band and red pimento for the bow. Serve on crisp lettuce with whipped mayonnaise. Serves 8.

CHILI STACK PARTY: When you go to Fort Worth to shop, scout around the delicatessens until you find dried black Mexican chili peppers. They look like bell peppers would look if all dried up and crisp. Buy 2 of these and a can of chili powder. (Of course if you can't find the peppers the chili powder will answer, but the flavor will not be the same nor will the sauce have the rich dark red color.)

For the rest, buy 1 large bunch of celery, 2 lbs. white onions, 2 lbs. corn meal, 2 lbs. ground steak, 2

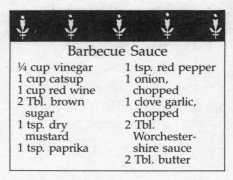

Barbecue Sauce

¼ cup vinegar	1 tsp. red pepper
1 cup catsup	1 onion,
1 cup red wine	chopped
2 Tbl. brown	1 clove garlic,
sugar	chopped
1 tsp. dry	2 Tbl.
mustard	Worchester-
1 tsp. paprika	shire sauce
	2 Tbl. butter

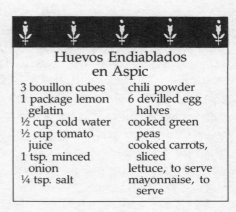

Huevos Endiablados en Aspic

3 bouillon cubes	chili powder
1 package lemon	6 devilled egg
gelatin	halves
½ cup cold water	cooked green
½ cup tomato	peas
juice	cooked carrots,
1 tsp. minced	sliced
onion	lettuce, to serve
¼ tsp. salt	mayonnaise, to
	serve

Ensalada Estilo Sombrero

2 cups cottage	green pepper
cheese	strips
1 tsp. salt	pimento strips
½ tsp. chili	lettuce, to serve
powder	whipped mayon-
pineapple juice	naise, to serve
8 pineapple	
slices	

Chili Stack Party

45-50 hoecakes, 4	2 lbs. yellow
inches in	cheese, grated
diameter	1 lb. white
Chili Stack sauce	onions,
	chopped fine

lbs. yellow cheese, and 4 cans tomatoes. (You'll have to beg, borrow, or steal the ration points!) Grapefruit salad is requisite with this, so get lettuce and 4 large grapefruits.

Make the **CHILI STACK SAUCE** the day before if possible: Put 4 cans tomatoes on to cook slowly with black chili peppers, rolled fine; celery, chopped fine; and 1 lb. onions, chopped. Cover and let cook for several hours. If the tomatoes simmer down to where there is very little juice, add a cup or 2 of water. Add to this 1 1¼-oz. can chili powder, 2 lbs. browned ground steak, and a garlic button (chopped), and let simmer until it is so thoroughly cooked it is like a thick smooth paste. Stir often. Salt to taste.

Use your red-checked gingham cloth and napkins and have your table set in buffet style. Some of those pine trees offer a very effective centerpiece of pine boughs and cones with a few red berries.

Now, the morning of your party, remove membranes from grapefruit with a sharp knife. Wash and crisp your lettuce, grate the cheese, chop the rest of your onions, and make about 45-50 corn meal hoecakes (see pg. 38) just as thin as possible and about 4 inches in diameter. Stack in a pan in warm oven until needed.

Just before supper, arrange your grapefruit on a platter of lettuce and have your French dressing (see pg. 19) ready.

Now, take any big, flat pan, a platter, or even the broiler pan in your oven and arrange 18 or 20 re-heated hoecakes on it so they do not touch. Have sauce piping hot and cover each cake with it. Sprinkle cheese over this and plenty of chopped onion. Then put on another cake and treat it the same way. Do this one more time, adding a big mountain of cheese to the top cake. Run this under the broiler long enough to melt the top cheese and take to table as is. I allowed 4 extra stacks for the four who always want an extra one. Serve with grapefruit salad and

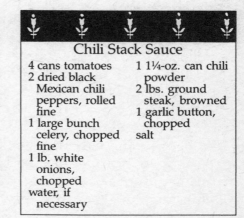

Chili Stack Sauce

4 cans tomatoes	1 1¼-oz. can chili powder
2 dried black Mexican chili peppers, rolled fine	2 lbs. ground steak, browned
1 large bunch celery, chopped fine	1 garlic button, chopped
1 lb. white onions, chopped	salt
water, if necessary	

coffee or beer. Pass around any extra hoecakes. Serves 12.

For 2 to 4 people, cut the recipe down to: 1 can tomatoes, 1 dried black Mexican pepper, 2 Tbl. chili powder, 2 stalks celery, 3 onions, 1 cup meal, ½ lb. ground steak, and ½ lb. cheese.

Bella suggests that I send our **WARTIME CHILI**, in case you are pushed for time. We keep several cans of chili and pork and beans on the pantry shelf all the time now, so that we can have chili at a moment's notice.

To 2 cans chili (without beans), add 1 can pork and beans and 2 Tbl. chili powder. Heat well and use as sauce for hoecakes, using same method as for enchiladas. Dick will love this, as it's so easy and inexpensive. This amount will serve 4 to 6.

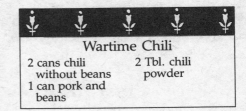

Wartime Chili

2 cans chili without beans	2 Tbl. chili powder
1 can pork and beans	

Love,
Mother

Atlanta, Georgia
April 2, 1943

Dearest Selma:

So at last you are going to have a place to plant
some flowers! That is something to be truly excited
over. I selected a few packages of seed for you today,
and will send full instructions for planting, and you
simply must plant every one. Who knows but what
you might have a *green hand*. Let Dick dig a little, or
drop in a seed, and from then on he'll be bragging
about *his* garden to all the neighboring gardeners.
No matter if you are moved again before the flowers
reach maturity, you will have had your fun watching
them and you will be able to leave a spot of beauty
behind you — which is a very nice gesture throughout life.

We are garden-minded here, too, and I can't wait
to get home in the afternoons to get my seed in.

Stewart writes in glowing terms of his life at New
River. He's just crazy about the Marines. Won't he
look handsome in his greens?!

It is so nice that you and Dick can keep the Colonel's baby so they can get out. I wish I could be a
sitter for the children of all those poor, tied-down
servicemen's wives. Sounds a little involved, but I'd
like to corral all the babies once a week so the par-
ents could get out for some well-deserved relaxa-
tion.

It must have made you and Dick feel like quite a
settled family to have a baby in the house. From
what you have told me, the Colonel's wife sounds
charming and friendly. It's so nice that you can be
neighbors.

I cannot resist sending you my recipes for molded
fruit or vegetable salad. It's so lovely for guests and
you seem to have plenty of those.

MOLDED VEGETABLE SALAD: If possible, get

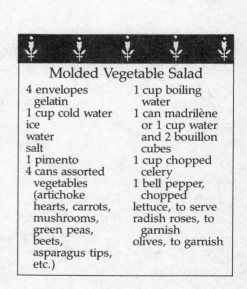

Molded Vegetable Salad

4 envelopes gelatin	1 cup boiling water
1 cup cold water	1 can madrilène
ice	or 1 cup water
water	and 2 bouillon
salt	cubes
1 pimento	1 cup chopped celery
4 cans assorted vegetables (artichoke hearts, carrots, mushrooms, green peas, beets, asparagus tips, etc.)	1 bell pepper, chopped
	lettuce, to serve
	radish roses, to garnish
	olives, to garnish

a can of madrilène for this, but if it isn't available, just use the faithful gelatin mixture with 2 bouillon cubes dissolved in it. I like to make this in one mold to serve everybody, because it looks so pretty. I suggest that you save this for your farewell buffet, as it will establish you as a real chef.

So dress your sweet self up and go shopping. Buy any canned vegetable that your points and your budget allow — English peas, hearts of artichoke, asparagus, button mushrooms, diced beets, diced carrots — not all of these, of course, but enough for variety in color and taste.

Then get a bell pepper and celery, a can of pimentos, a new package of gelatin, and a can of madrilène, and you are ready. If the mold I sent you last Christmas is not in storage, use it, but if it is not present, then use any big bowl or 3-qt. boiler with a nice shape. Rinse it out in cold water. Put on your gayest apron for this; it is a real adventure.

Now put about 2 cups water on to boil and put 4 envelopes gelatine to soak in 1 cup cold water. Select a flat pan that will hold the mold and have lots of room left. Take 2 pans of ice from the refrigerator and put it in your flat pan. (I use my biscuit pan.) Pour a little water over the ice and sprinkle it with salt, placing your mold in the midst of the ice and water to get cold.

Now open your cans of vegetables and drain, and arrange some of them in a design on the bottom of the mold. I cut a pimento into strips and spread it out in the center of the mold. It looks just like a Mexican sunflower. Put a border of artichokes, peas, or carrots all around the edge. Inside these, put a row of button mushrooms, green peas, or beets (if beets, be sure to wash thoroughly so the red juice won't spread). Just work out the prettiest design possible with what you have. I've never made it the same way twice. Now stand asparagus tips or stips of bell pepper up around the sides of the mold.

Pour a cup of boiling water over your soaked gelatin and stir until it dissolves. Add the can of madrilène or another cup of water. Stir well and here comes the fun. With a spoon, slowly and carefully put some of this mixture into the mold over the design. Use sparingly, for if too much is used the vegetables will float and ruin your handiwork. Just a few teaspoonfuls at the time, so it will jell as it settles down into the cold mold. Now, don't hurry. While this hardens, open the other ends of your cans, step on them, and drop them in your tin can box for the war effort. You can also straighten up the table and wash any dishes sitting around. Now, put in more gelatin. It should be firm enough. Shake the mold very gently and test it. This time you can put in about ½ inch of gelatin. While that gets firm, wash your celery and chop it up (about a cup). Chop the bell pepper and the rest of the pimentos.

Mix these with all the other vegetables you have — enough to fill the mold. When the mixture is firm again, and at least 1-inch deep, gently place the rest of the vegetables on top of the firm gelatin, being careful to keep the asparagus standing up like soldiers. When the mold is filled, take the trusty spoon and pour the gelatin all around the side so the asparagus will have plenty around it and then pour the rest in until the mold is full. Set this in the ice box and in a few hours it will be ready to use. I always like to make this the night before, so that on the day of my party there is more time for other chores.

When you are ready to serve this, dip your mold just *1 or 2 seconds* in hot water. Too long and your picture melts. Turn it out on a lettuce-filled platter. Garnish with radish roses and olives. It is beautiful and so professional looking. You'll be the proudest hostess! Just remember to use an extra envelope of gelatin and let the design set before you proceed. Its a cinch. Serves 12 to 16.

For **MOLDED FRUIT SALAD**, use exactly the same procedure, but you'll find it even more fascinating because you can use the pimento sunflower

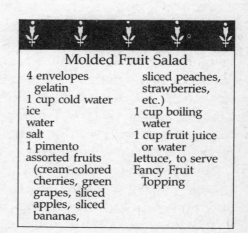

Molded Fruit Salad

4 envelopes gelatin	sliced peaches, strawberries, etc.)
1 cup cold water	1 cup boiling water
ice	
water	1 cup fruit juice or water
salt	
1 pimento	lettuce, to serve
assorted fruits (cream-colored cherries, green grapes, sliced apples, sliced bananas,	Fancy Fruit Topping

and cream colored cherries or green grapes in your design and fill the mold with any fruit you desire. Use fruit juice or water in the gelatin instead of madrilène. But — and here's the out-of-this-world touch — for a **FANCY FRUIT TOPPING**, whip some coffee cream, add a few spoonfuls of mayonnaise and a dash of crème de menthe or wine, and serve with your fruit mold for a truly elegant treat.

Here are a few more ideas for **HORS D'OEUVRES**: Stuff olives with anchovy paste or anchovy fillets. Spread caviar on small thin slices of toast and cover with grated hard-boiled egg. Cut a raw cauliflower into flowerettes and serve with a cocktail sauce or mayonnaise with a little curry powder added. Mix cream cheese with sardines, anchovy paste, or chives and serve with potato chips. Serve any kind of snappy cheese and crackers. Roll a tid-bit of American cheese in chipped beef and serve on toothpicks.

Be sure to have your crackers and potato chips crisp and fresh. Run them in the oven at the last minute, if necessary, to crisp them. Arrange your platters attractively. The food will disappear like magic.

To make **GLAZED APPLES**: Select medium or small red or green apples which are firm and tart. Core and peel. Make a syrup in small boiler of 1 cup sugar and 1 cup water with enough red vegetable coloring to make a deep red. When this has cooked 10 minutes, drop in 2 or 3 apples without crowding, and turn often so the coloring will be even. Do not stick a fork in them. When apples are done they should be tender, with a pretty, glazed surface. Remove to plate to cool. Put in more apples to cook. Makes 6 apples. Use these around meats. They may be made green by using green vegetable coloring.

Steaks are such rare treats these days that I feel it useless to give you many instructions about them. Of course you know how to pan-broil a steak. Porterhouse, club, and loin are the only cuts to broil.

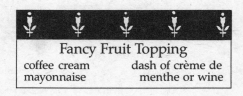

Fancy Fruit Topping

coffee cream	dash of crème de
mayonnaise	menthe or wine

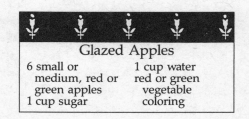

Glazed Apples

6 small or	1 cup water
medium, red or	red or green
green apples	vegetable
1 cup sugar	coloring

PAN-BROILED STEAK: Be sure to have your skillet red hot, and smear it over with a piece of the fat off the steak. Never use butter or grease of any other kind. Sear it on one side — turn quickly and sear on other side. This seals in the juices. Never lower heat and never cover — broil fast. Cook about 5 minutes on each side for rare steaks.

Salt after removing steak to platter. Remember, any liquid or butter, or steam or salt will draw the juices out of your steak and leave a grand gravy, but a hunk of fiber!

If you think your steak may not be of the best quality, trim it up about an hour before you want to cook it. Cut several slant-wise slits across it and squeeze lemon juice over it. This tenderizes it and adds greatly to the flavor, but do not tamper with a fine steak.

Why not teach Dick to broil the steaks? Men love to do it and take great pride in their method. I've tried all the men's ways and find this the best but Dick will add variations in his sauces. Personally, I feel that any sauce ruins a *good* steak.

Lots of love,
Mother

Atlanta, Georgia
April 29, 1943

Selma darling:

Your wire announcing the removal of Dick's squadron to San Diego so suddenly has an ominous note, as it sounds so much like a port of call. But Daddy says I'm just borrowing trouble, so I shall pretend that it is just another stopover in your National Cook's Tour.

The wire gave no indication of sadness over leaving your darling lakeside home — the huge fireplace for cool evenings and the treasured friends you have both made on Eagle Mountain Lake — but I know it was hard to "take up your bed and walk."

Your generation is learning so many valuable lessons in character-building that I tremble for fear that when the war is over and you all come marching triumphantly home, you'll find us older folks rather inadequate and weak. Of course, we did come along during another war and we've had depressions and booms and now more war, but even at that, we haven't been uprooted every few months and we haven't had to adjust ourselves to such infinitely changing conditions.

So please, when the war is over, don't look upon us as spoiled old fogies. Remember we've tried to do the best we could even though our understanding is limited, perhaps, since the even tenor of our actual living conditions has been so little disturbed. I am trying to develop stamina and courage to enable me to meet whatever arises, but I find myself slipping backward into a soft-hearted, sentimental, emotional mother instead of going forward in the role of brave soldier.

The fact that Dick wants you to serve our frozen punches with your meat courses proves beyond any doubt that his confidence in your culinary ability is boundless. I would never have suggested such an added expense and trouble to a new housekeeper,

but Dick is quite right. There isn't any other touch you can give a company dinner that adds so much glamour.

It may be too late to send these recipes, since you may not find a place to keep house in San Diego (I hear it is horribly crowded), but I shall tell you how to make them and Dick can look forward to having them later if not now.

We never serve **ROSE PUNCH** unless we have a choice pink rose to place on each little dessert plate. It would be like a dance without music! Having such lovely roses all spring and summer and even until the first frost in November, we do not have to deny ourselves this treat except during the winter months, but I'm wondering where you will find pink rosebuds.

Once you have the roses, look to your glassware, for this treat should be served in a glass tulip cup or punch cup on a glass plate with a finger bowl mat under the cup. Serve with your meat course or between meat course and salad if you are serving in courses (as you may do if an era of maids ever returns).

Make a syrup of 1 cup sugar and 1 cup water and boil 5 minutes. Let cool and pour over stiffly beaten whites of 2 eggs; add 3 or 4 drops of oil of roses and place in pan in ice box to freeze. This should be frozen in an hour or 2. Serves 6.

Another way we make it is to add 4 mashed bananas to syrup before pouring over eggs — this makes a richer ice and also needs another drop or 2 of oil of roses.

In winter, when roses no longer bloom in the garden, we like **CRANBERRY ICE** with fowl or roast beef. This is better made in a freezer, but Dick will never know the difference if it is frozen in ice box. Serve it in glass also.

Cook 1 cup sugar, 1 cup water, and 2 cups cranber-

Rose Punch

1 cup sugar	3 or 4 drops of
1 cup water	oil of roses
2 egg whites,	pink rosebuds,
stiffly beaten	to garnish

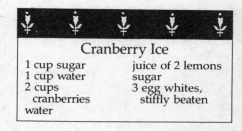

Cranberry Ice

1 cup sugar	juice of 2 lemons
1 cup water	sugar
2 cups	3 egg whites,
cranberries	stiffly beaten
water	

ries until the berries are soft enough to mash through a strainer. Measure the juice, and add an equal amount of water and the juice of 2 lemons. Taste, and if not sweet enough, add more sugar, remembering it will lose some of its sweetness in freezing. Fold in the stiffly beaten whites of 3 eggs and set in tray to freeze. Serves 8.

Here is another delicious frozen punch for fowl or meat. I call it **THREE OF A KIND PUNCH**. Grate the rinds of 1 lemon and 1 orange. Squeeze juice of each and add to grated rind. Mash 1 banana and add to juice. Mix with 1 cup water and 1 cup sugar and freeze. A sprig of mint in each glass adds to this. Especially so, if you put 1 tsp. crème de menthe on top of the ice! Serves 4.

Daddy says that Dick is a man's man — just because he likes my **BUTTERMILK ICE CREAM**! Aren't men funny — but it is good, and not too rich to serve after a heavy meal.

To 1 qt. buttermilk (and you might as well make a quart because he'll want more before he retires), add the juice and grated rind of 3 lemons or limes. Add 1 cup sugar and stir until dissolved. Put in freezing pan and allow 3 hours to freeze, stirring twice. Green maraschino cherries top this off nicely.

The **PISTACHIO SALAD** is nothing but a box of lime gelatin. Pour over this 2 cups boiling water and stir until dissolved. Add 1 cup chopped pistachio meats, 1 cup chopped celery, and the juice of 1 lemon, and put in mold to congeal. Serves 4.

Here's the **CHEESE BALL SALAD** you asked for — yes, it's quite pretty and good too. Mash 2 3-oz. cream cheeses, and add enough mayonnaise to soften slightly. Mix in 1 cup nuts and 1 small can chopped pimentos. Roll into little balls, after first putting paprika on the palm of your hands. Serve heaped up on lettuce or watercress or on nasturtium leaves, using a nasturtium flower for a festive touch. Serves 6.

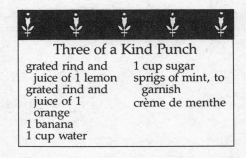

Three of a Kind Punch

grated rind and juice of 1 lemon	1 cup sugar
grated rind and juice of 1 orange	sprigs of mint, to garnish
1 banana	crème de menthe
1 cup water	

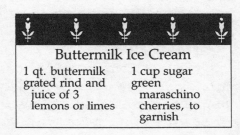

Buttermilk Ice Cream

1 qt. buttermilk	1 cup sugar
grated rind and juice of 3 lemons or limes	green maraschino cherries, to garnish

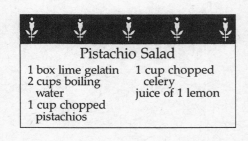

Pistachio Salad

1 box lime gelatin	1 cup chopped celery
2 cups boiling water	juice of 1 lemon
1 cup chopped pistachios	

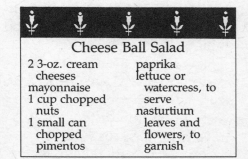

Cheese Ball Salad

2 3-oz. cream cheeses	paprika
mayonnaise	lettuce or watercress, to serve
1 cup chopped nuts	nasturtium leaves and flowers, to garnish
1 small can chopped pimentos	

I had not sent you our recipe for **MERINGUES**, because I could not imagine you aspiring to be so fancy, but here it is: Beat 4 egg whites stiff (add ½ tsp. cream of tartar to them first). Fold in 6 Tbl. sugar (added gradually), flavor with 1 tsp. vanilla extract, and drop on greased wax paper on a biscuit tin in large spoonfuls. With a spoon, make a nice cavity in the center of each, leaving the edges piled high. Bake 1 hour in 225° oven — these should just dry out and not brown. They should be cooked through and be crisp. When done, turn off oven, open door, and allow to cool in oven 10 minutes. Of course, we use our pastry tube and do very fancy stunts, but wait until the war is over before you bother. You may make them pink or green with vegetable coloring added to egg whites. When cold, put these on dessert plates and heap ice cream in centers. This recipe makes 12 3-inch meringues or 1 9-inch pie shell.

Do you remember when we used to make our meringues lavender, flavor custard ice cream with violet, and decorate with candied violets? What festive days, those, when a dessert could assume such vast importance! Never mind, darling, the time will come when you will think such things worthy of your meticulous attention. You may even want to freeze an orchid in a cake of ice to use in place of finger bowls — just wipe your fingers daintily on the ice and there you are!

But frozen orchids are a long way from telling you how to use **BEET TOPS**. I'm delighted that you asked about this because it shows a thrifty trend and you'll like them.

Whenever you buy beets having fresh red leaves, cut them 2 inches from the beets and wash them several times. Cut into pieces and cook in small amount of water with 1 Tbl. sugar and 1 Tbl. butter. If leaves are young, they should cook in 30 to 40 minutes. A dash of vinegar improves these.

MY SPAGHETTI: This spaghetti is very easy, but it too calls for tomatoes. Of course, when you had

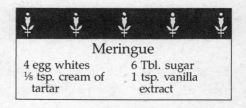

Meringue

4 egg whites	6 Tbl. sugar
⅛ tsp. cream of tartar	1 tsp. vanilla extract

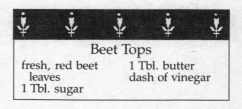

Beet Tops

fresh, red beet leaves	1 Tbl. butter
	dash of vinegar
1 Tbl. sugar	

My Spaghetti

1 No. 2 can tomatoes	1 Tbl. chili powder
1 can water	1 box spaghetti
1 bell pepper, chopped	salt
1 onion, chopped	2 Tbl. cornstarch
several stalks of celery, chopped	½ cup water
1 garlic button, chopped	chopped onions
butter	grated Parmesan cheese
½-1 lb. round steak, ground	

spaghetti suppers here at home, we used six cans of tomatoes and four boxes of spaghetti, but you can have it any time you can find *one* can of tomatoes.

Put 1 No. 2 can tomatoes and 1 can water on to heat in large boiler. Chop a bell pepper, an onion, several stalks of celery, and a garlic button, and put into tomatoes. Brown in butter in skillet 1 lb. (or ½ lb.) ground round steak. Add to tomatoes with 1 Tbl. chili powder and let simmer a long, long time, until sauce is thick and dark. Add more water if it cooks down too thick.

Thirty minutes before supper, drop spaghetti (1 box) into boiling, salted water and cook until tender. Drain and pile on platter.

Bind sauce with 2 Tbl. cornstarch rubbed smooth in water. When thick, pour over spaghetti on platter. Sprinkle chopped onions over this and add a heavy coating of grated Parmesan cheese.

If this sauce is made the day before, it is better, but if made early in the morning, it is very good. The trick is to let it cook until it gets *dark* red and pulpy before serving. Serves 4 to 6.

Mama was quite pleased that Dick said he had to have Sally Lunn before he left this country, and strawberry shortcake just like she made it. Well, I don't blame him.

MAMA'S SALLY LUNN: Beat 2 egg whites together until very light. Add 2 Tbl. sugar and beat some more. Sift 2½ cups flour with 1 tsp. salt and 4 tsp. baking powder. Sift this into the eggs, stirring until well mixed, and then pour in ¼ cup melted butter. Pour into 2 layer cake pans which have been greased. Cook in preheated 425° oven until brown (about 30 minutes). Place 1 layer on platter and pour ¼ cup melted butter over it. Place second layer on this and pour ¼ cup melted butter over top. Serve piping hot, cut into wedges like pie or cake.

STRAWBERRY SHORTCAKE: Make Baking

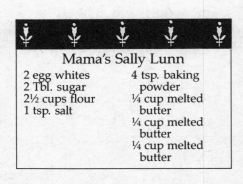

Mama's Sally Lunn

2 egg whites	4 tsp. baking
2 Tbl. sugar	powder
2½ cups flour	¼ cup melted
1 tsp. salt	butter
	¼ cup melted
	butter
	¼ cup melted
	butter

Strawberry Shortcake

Baking Powder	sweetened
Biscuits	whipped cream
strawberries,	
slightly mashed	
and sweetened	

Powder Biscuits (see pg. 7), and cut out ¼-inch thick with large biscuit cutter. Butter each one, using pastry brush, and put one biscuit on top of another one until you have a pair for each person to be served. Bake in preheated 450° oven 12-15 minutes.

When done, remove upper biscuit. Place lower one on dessert plate, and cover with strawberries, slightly mashed and sweetened. Put top biscuit on this and add more strawberries. Top with sweetened whipped cream and serve immediately. When cake is used for shortcake, it must be served cold. Biscuits may also be served cold.

Neither Bella nor I are sure which ground steak dish Dick referred to, but I believe it must have been the **CHESTNUT STEAK** I invented the night he flew up from Pensacola and I was put to it to make two pounds of ground steak turn into a company dish to serve four extra people. We had a pound of boiled chestnuts which we were going to have creamed but they would not have been enough to go around, and I found a half box of fresh mushrooms on the back porch.

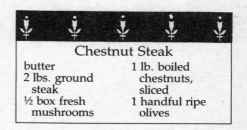

Chestnut Steak

butter	1 lb. boiled
2 lbs. ground	chestnuts,
steak	sliced
½ box fresh	1 handful ripe
mushrooms	olives

So I put some butter in the skillet and put in the ground steak, stirring it around until it was all browned. I sliced and broiled the mushrooms in another pan, and later added them to the steak. Then the boiled chestnuts were sliced and dumped in, and then, not quite satisfied, I sliced a handful of ripe olives into the mixture and stirred it all together.

I piled it, steaming hot, on the round silver platter, garnishing with rice molds, and made a gravy from the luscious juices and butter left in the pan after I had taken up the steak. I hope this is the one Dick wants. I remember at the time he said it was the best thing he ever tasted — but that may have been because he was so much in love. Serves 8.

I'm writing from the office and left your last letter at home, so I'm not sure I've covered the ground. If

not, the other requested recipes will come later. Am sending this to your Eagle Mountain address, hoping it will be forwarded. I can't wait to hear how you are situated in San Diego, and if "Old Matilda" stood up under the trip.

I must say that I never dreamed my own daughter would become like the proverbial "traveling man!" But this is indeed a generation of traveling women!

All love,
Mother

Atlanta, Georgia
May 10, 1943

Selma darling:

Your letter arrived this morning, after I had spent a frantic week of waiting to know if you had found a bed upon which to rest your weary bones. Such a relief to know you found one, even though it does have to disappear into the wall during the day! I think you were lucky to find even one room, much less a kitchenette as "big as a thimble."

I see no reason for not having friends in — you'll be so lonely if you don't — but I would suggest having only two or three at a time. You know people like to be comfortable, so be sure the chairs will go around — a bridge table only seats four comfortably! And keep refreshments very simple. A bun is a feast when garnished with smiles!

I am much too excited today to write recipes. Your darling little poem, announcing that I will be a Grandmother before many months, had me in a trance all day, and when I phoned Daddy and read it to him he said, "Well, I might just as well close up the office and come home!" He added that he thought it would be wonderful to be a Grandfather but he'd be darned if he liked the idea of being married to a Grandmother! Now, isn't that just like a man?

Seriously darling, I've never been so thrilled in all my life, and I haven't been able to keep tears from streaming down my cheeks. Tears of happiness, of course, thinking of all the joys to come; but tears of sadness too, because of you being so far away from me, shut off in that tiny room among strangers in a strange city. I ache to see you, to know exactly how you feel, to know that you are taking care of yourself.

Be sure to drink lots of milk and eat fruits, and rest all you can. Take Dick out for dinner some and take a holiday from cooking. Spend hours lying down reading a good book or just daydreaming. Plan

exquisite little garments we can make. Keep your mind filled with pleasant thoughts.

What variety of baby does Dick think he wants? Most men want a son first and I don't know why, because they never go as insane over a son as they do a daughter. Perhaps its just a matter of pride, a hand-me-down from royalty.

I cannot wait to go layette shopping! Oh, it's all just so exciting and thrilling I can't settle down to anything, and so I dash around like the proverbial chicken with his head cut off.

Bella is very suspicious and hurt because I have not told her what was in your letter. She knows from my antics that it is something of paramount importance, but somehow I just want to hold the secret close to my heart awhile!

I know that Dick is so puffed up with pride that he just goes around grinning all the time. Don't think for a moment that you can keep it a secret — he'll tell every man in the squadron before the week is over. Tell him to keep his feet on the ground — even when he's flying!

Ten years ago Daniel Whitehead Hicky wrote a sonnet which I think you'd do well to adopt these days. Its a far cry from the prosaic recipes I've been sending you, and should be a relief.

> Spread sunlight on his toast, and spread it
> thickly,
> And have it not too brown, and then upon it
> Drop powdered violet petals on it lightly,
> quickly
> While mentally he works upon a sonnet.
> For luncheon he must have delphinium broth,
> Chilled water-lily salad and a rose;
> Or give him Shasta daisy hearts, or both —
> And bluebells will ring luncheon to a close.
> Move quietly through the household. Never
> speak
> Of pots and pans; talk only of the moon,

Of amber twilights and cool woods that reek
With fragrances of rain. Sing him a tune
And ask him softly each fall of dew:
"One star dropped in your tea, my dear, or
two?"

> With all love in the world
> to the future parents of
> the world's cutest baby,
> Mother

P.S. Stewart called tonight to say that he was leaving
for the West Coast but does not know where
he's going. Ward has been transferred to Phila-
delphia. He has found a tiny apartment for
Sarah and Elizabeth. John and Bec are in Macon
still.

Atlanta, Georgia
June 1, 1943

My dear, darling Selma:

You may tell from this salutation that I am again simply drooling sentiment, but it is frankly unashamed. If you hadn't written so bravely about Dick's assignment overseas, I could have behaved with more dignity and restraint. *Squadron Leader* — how wonderful that sounds, but when I think what it means, I quake with shame at my weakness compared with your courage and strength of character. Dive bombers! And Dick out there in the front leading them in.

My first reaction to the news was one of unbounded pride. Pride that my daughter had won so fine a man and pride that Dick is capable of filling a position of such paramount importance to his country. My second reaction was one of anxiety for you, which I have no right to voice, but which tears at my heart strings. For him to leave now when you aren't well anyway just seems so hard. Of course, I shall do all in my power to keep you happy and busy, but I know how long and lonely some hours will be. I'll say this for you, Selma, "You're a better man than I am, Gunga Din!"

I try to make excuses for my happiness at the thought of you coming home by telling myself that after all, I am a very average mother who has missed her eldest daughter since she married. The old adage about the ill wind is certainly applicable here because in my wildest dreams I could not have imagined that a horrible, tragic world war could bring any good thing to anybody. Much less that it would bring me the privilege of having my first grandchild here in my own home day after day to love and cherish, and to have you too — well, "my cup runneth over." I realize what a selfish viewpoint this is but believe me, darling, I'm going to grab and hold any break I get in this global war and thank the dear Lord for what good things come my way.

I envy Dick — just as I envy all the able-bodied

140

men who are fated to have an active part in this war. Dick is strong and young, well trained, capable, and happy in his job in this, the greatest debacle the world has ever known. Dick will face the thing squarely and follow through with gallantry. I shall wrap him securely in a thick blanket of prayer where no Japanese bullet may penetrate and he will come back when Victory is won.

He's going to miss you, and your sweet ways — and your cooking! He's going to miss America and all it stands for, but he's going out to fight a good fight and come home. And we'll be so busy we won't know time is flying by, and we'll have something to show him when he comes sailing home! I'm resigning from war work, because there are plenty of women who can do that job, but I cannot let anyone else be with you each day or raise my grandchild. I have inherited that pleasure and I wonder what I've done to deserve it!

I think it was simply wonderful that you and Dick could ride up to see Stewart at Camp Pendleton last Sunday. He was so thrilled to see you both. He called Monday night and seemed so happy, but was not sure just how many days he has before he will leave. He's been assigned (as he probably told you) to a Replacement Battalion. He was right cute; he said he was the most *private* private in the Service! Bless his heart — he's so young and so fine — well, that's another bridge to cross, but I hope you'll get home before he sails to help me cross it.

Am so glad you were able to get plane reservations, and I do pray they won't put you off in a desert somewhere. If the baby is a girl we'll have to teach her to cook in her infancy, as it's the only interval in which she'll have time until she marries. Wire me when and where to meet you, and until then, Darling, just hold everything!

Love from,
Mother

Index

144

148